CHURCH GROWTH AND GROUP CONVERSION

BY

BISHOP J. W. PICKETT, DR. A. L. WARNSHUIS,
REV. G. H. SINGH, DR. D. A. McGAVRAN

FOREWORD BY JOHN R. MOTT

~◊~

Dedicated to those men and women
who labor for the growth of the Churches,
discarding theories of church growth which do not work
and learning and practicing productive patterns which
actually disciple the peoples and increase
the Household of God

~◊~

William Carey Library

Library of Congress Card Catalog Number 73-80163
International Standard Book Number 0-87808-712-5

First Edition,   1936
Second Edition,   1938
Third Edition,   1956
Fourth Edition,   1962
Fifth Edition,   1973

The 1973 edition was published by the
William Carey Library
533 Hermosa Street
South Pasadena, Calif.
91030

PRINTED IN THE UNITED STATES OF AMERICA

1629

BV
652.25
C561
1973

CONTENTS

Foreword

Preface

FOREWORD

THE distinctive and important contribution of this most instructive, stimulating and reassuring book has been that of setting forth with clarity and frankness why on the one hand the work of so many churches and mission stations has been so comparatively sterile, and why in other cases their labors have been attended with wonderful fruitfulness. It raises the serious question whether the time has not come in field after field, not only in India but also in other lands, when there should be a major shift in emphasis and a marked reallocation of resources of men and money.

September 27th, 1937   JOHN R. MOTT
Chairman of the International
Missionary Council, New York, U.S.A.

PREFACE TO THIRD EDITION

THIS book is a collection of early writings on church growth and group conversion. Chapters III to IX are a revision of a pioneer study in Mid-India where very slow increase of the churches and heavy institutionalism has been characteristic of most missions. The study arose out of widespread dissatisfaction among Indian church leaders and missionaries with this situation.

In 1931 the Christian community connected with the Protestant Church in Mid-India numbered about 58,000 souls. In 134 of the area's 145 mission stations the rate of increase for 1921-31 averaged 12%,—less than the normal birth rate. In the remaining stations the rate of increase was 200% and indicated that the Church was growing healthily through adult conversions. However, since the eleven stations were for the most part remote and their increases unknown, the general impression among the Christian leadership of the area was that the growth of the churches must necessarily be very slow. So much so that even those whose churches were achieving great growth were dubious as to its soundness!

Then in 1933 came J. W. Pickett's epochal book "Christian Mass Movements in India." It marked a turning point in mission history. To leaders convinced that Christianization is necessarily a very slow and difficult process, Dr. Pickett's accounts of the triumphs of the Gospel and of its redemptive power in areas where men had accepted it in the people movement fashion caused a revolution in thinking. Leaders realized that while

much of Mid-India seemed sterile, still there were occurring and had occurred numerous group conversions similar
in nature to the movements which led to the establishment of the great churches in Chhota Nagpur and the
Andhra country. The Mid-India Provincial Christian
Council made provision for investigation into the possibility
of church growth in Mid-India. Dr. Pickett's services were
secured and Mr. Singh and Dr. McGavran were appointed as his helpers.

Two kinds of areas were selected for study. First those
in which the 200% church growth was being achieved.
Second those in which there was hope that people movement growth might be induced if special efforts were made.
The purpose was to determine how and why people movements start, how they have been arrested, why they die,
what mission procedures conduce to sterility and what
make for great growth.

The studies by Pickett, Singh and McGavran were first
published under the title "Christian Missions in Mid-India"
in 1936. The book was an immediate success. Dr. J. F.
Edwards of the Congregational Church, editor of the
West India "Gnyanodaya" called the book "A veritable
masterpiece on evangelism," and said, "If we had the
money we would send a free copy to every Indian Christian
leader who knows English and to every missionary in India,
trusting that he would be moved, and searched, and
inspired, as we ourselves have been." A second edition
with a foreword by Dr. John R. Mott was published in
1938. Today renewed interest demands a reprinting of
these pioneer insights into church growth and mission
procedures. This third edition condenses the book,widens
its application, adds a chapter by a well-known author

and changes the title to the more precise "Church Growth and Group Conversion."

The first two editions used the term 'mass movement' to describe caste-wise ingathering. It has now been seen that the term 'people movement' more accurately and meaningfully describes what actually occurs in that kind of ingathering. So, with the kind permission of my fellow authors, I have substituted it for the earlier term.

Rev. G. H. Singh's contribution to this volume lies in his valuable services as a member of the visiting team of 1936 and his editorial comment on the drafts prepared by other members. Both he and I wish to emphasize the large part played in our thought by Bishop Pickett's creative and original insights. We are among the many who lit our candles at his fire.

In the years that followed Bishop Pickett's publications on the sound church growth to be achieved through people movements to Christ, other missionary statesmen described aspects of this dynamic type of missions. Dr. A. L. Warnshuis of the International Missionary Council, one of the great leaders of missions in America during the last forty years, set forth two ways of achieving church growth in stratified non-Christian nations: the wrong way by the conversion of individuals extracted from a dozen different peoples; and the better way "by recognition of the principle that the Church grows along racial lines in social strata." Dr. Warnshuis' fine statement, first published in 1942, becomes our Chapter II to underline the fact that, although the rest of the book illustrates church growth from India, *group conversion from within one people applies all round the world.* Peoples move into Christian faith, or refuse to do so, in accordance with certain general principles. Dr. Warnshuis describes some of these in terms applicable to land after land. We hope that "Church Growth and Group Conversion" will prove useful throughout the world wherever the Christian World Mission faces non-growing mission station churches. The book presents a series of case studies and will be found replete with lessons for all who desire the multiplication and welfare of the Church.

We trust that none will fall victim to the idea that this book, being a revision of one published eighteen years ago, is 'years behind the times.' *The principles underlying the Indian case histories presented are timeless and apply to many lands.* At least three fourths of the great growth of the Churches today, in most non-occidental lands, is taking place in country after country along the lines described in this book. Indeed, the Church today cannot be correctly understood apart from understanding its chief mode of expansion.

DONALD McGAVRAN,
Missions House
Yale Divinity School
New Haven, Conn. U.S.A.

May 1955

PREFACE TO FOURTH EDITION

CONTINUING demand indicates that this book speaks to a wide need. Some missionaries and ministers, not having seen group conversions and people movements, find the concepts and methods difficult to understand. Others wonder if group conversion is biblically permissible.

These case studies of six beginning people movements, each involving group conversion and each fathered by a different denomination, illustrate several kinds of group conversion — or multi-individual conversion as it is called today. The three chapters on theory illuminate the matter still further. The reader sees what kinds of evangelistic effort assist group conversion and what kinds prevent it.

Both kinds will be seen to be natural and, given the circumstances, reasonable. Consider those efforts which prevent people movements from occurring. The national ministers and missionaries concerned did the best they knew. Their actions seemed to them entirely reasonable. We say to ourselves, "If we had been in their places, we would have done the same things." Consider also the actions which encouraged group conversions. These are described in historical detail. We can see them occurring. We stand with the leaders deciding to do those things which furthered them. And thus understand the process better.

As we look back on those events, we can learn much from them. As we look forward, we can avoid making the same mistakes and can copy the rewarding actions. This book has been written to enable a more effective evangelism, a more successful church planting, and many more vigorous and evangelistically potent Churches.

As the world mission gathers power, missionaries from Europe and America — and from Asia, Africa, and Latin America also — will stream out to lands of open doors and to the evangelization of the world. Many of these missionaries, I trust, will find these studies in church growth of value.

Donald McGavran

March first 1973   *School of Missions, Fuller Seminary, Pasadena, California, 91101, U.S.A.*

I

THE PEOPLE MOVEMENT POINT OF VIEW

Donald McGavran

A CROSS the world today in practically every non-Occidental country numerous people movements to Christ are going on. Some are making good progress producing strong churches. Some are limping along producing weak churches. Some have stopped. Some have even died.

These movements are seldom fully understood even by the church leaders and missionaries who tend them, because they are seen in the framework of individualistic church growth so characteristic of the West. They are therefore frequently unrecognized and mishandled.

The people movement point of view describes these movements, defines their essential nature, defends them as being a valid, common, and significant mode of church growth. It seeks to correct the common misunderstandings concerning them and to focus attention on them as an important highway of the spirit along which Christ is advancing to the heart of the nations.

Elements of the people movement point of view have repeatedly been stated, but usually in connection with some particular work, as if they were special light on a unique situation. The tribal nature of Christian ingathering during the conversion of Europe is frequently described—as a regrettable peculiarity of church expansion in Europe. Some missionaries in Africa have seen

the importance of like speaking to like, but have considered it a process peculiar to their section of Africa.
Even Pickett's tremendous assessment of the people movements in India, while it awakened very wide interest and
was actually the key to a world-wide statement, was held
to mark "the beginning of a new epoch in work on behalf
of the oppressed classes in India." The synthesis which
united in a consistent whole the various elements of people
movement methodology around the world had not been
made in 1938. The studies here reprinted are part of the
evidence[1] out of which the synthesis stated in world terms
was emerging.

The people movement point of view is to a certain
extent opposed by a traditional static point of view which
we call the "mission station approach" or the "central station tradition." This latter has grown up during the last
hundred and fifty years in which missions have been
making their slow, inch by inch progress in the face of
resistant non-Christian cultures. While there have been,
indeed, the people movement responses mentioned in our
first paragraph, successful ones of which have left congregations all across a countryside, the characteristic response to mission effort has been a rejection of the Gospel,
leaving static congregations chiefly at mission stations. A
great deal of mission work has consisted in the presentation
of the Gospel, by all the means which love could devise to
serve in the name of the Savior and to induce a fair
consideration of His claims—in the face of continuing

---

1   Essential to understanding the people movement point of view and
providing some of the buttressing evidence and most of the original
insight are Eishop J. Waskom Pickett's two influential books which
all should have: "Christ's Way to India's Heart," and "Christian
Mass Movements in India," 1934 and 1936. The former is available
from The Lucknow Publishing House, Lucknow, U. P., India.

rejection of the Christian religion. Such mission work has produced not only extremely slow church growth, but also a philosophy of missions to suit. Conditioned by the slow growth, this philosophy has developed its own dicta of what constitutes "good missions," of how slowly the younger Churches must grow, of how permeation of non-Christian cultures was as good an end as church establishment, and of how much philanthropy should be mixed with how much evangelism to insure a continuation of the mission in a non-Christian civilization. This static philosophy and methodology of missions reigns supreme in many places. It is seldom questioned or, for that matter, exposed to view. It is taken for granted. It is the unconscious ground of most missionary thinking. It is quite willing to accept people movements as an unusual and somewhat questionable form of mission work found here and there, and to be supported equally with all other types of mission work as far as funds can be stretched. But it is reluctant to concede that people movements to Christian faith are a normal way in which peoples come to Christian faith and constitute, wherever they occur, the pearls of great price. Hence the people movement point of view is by some called one-sided or partisan. However, there are many who earnestly long for clues to great and sound church growth. Thus despite the vested interests of the mission station approach, the people movement position is being welcomed as what it claims to be, not the only mode of church growth but a widespread mode of the greatest importance to those seeking the extension of Christ's Kingdom.

Readers may find the term "people movement" unfamiliar. By it we mean church growth which has variously been called mass movements, revivals and group movements. We shall not use the term "mass movement" and urge others not to use it. It is misleading. It does give some idea of the numbers involved, but fails completely to indicate that the movement (a) is not one of mere mass, but always of a people (tribe, caste, or clan); (b) usually enlarges by the conversion of small, well-instructed groups; and (c) achieves large numbers only over a period of years.

We do occasionally use the term "revival," but not often; because in the lands of the West, it means church growth from among a discipled people or nation, and also because it is possible to have a revival with no membership increase whatever. Great church growth from among non-Christian peoples is certainly a work of the Holy Spirit, but in the interests of understanding how the Holy Spirit works, it must not usually be called a revival. We shall occasionally use the term "group movement," but not often because there have been so many group movements within the older churches. The term "group conversion from within one people" is accurate but unwieldy. It will be shortened to "group conversion" and often used. It appears in our title.

Our principal term, however, is "people movement" because we are describing the way in which a people (tribe, caste, or clan) first becomes Christian. Caste movement, tribe movement, clan movement—these terms are accurate, but the single term "people movement" covers all three and hence is used. When the Church has multiplied greatly it has frequently grown in people movement fashion. For example, the New Testament Church was for years a one people movement. It grew strictly within the

Jews for a dozen years before it jumped to other peoples.

Another term used is "an approachable people." Approachability does not mean merely that the people in question is friendly, can be addressed, or listens to the Gospel; but that some of its sub-groups are actually accepting Jesus our Lord, being baptized and formed into congregations. On the basis of this kind of response, we judge that we have an "approachable people."

Basic to the entire point of view is the concept of a people. A people is a society whose members marry exclusively within it. Whether such a caste or tribe is really racially distinct from others is immaterial. As long as its sons take wives only from the people itself, so long will it think of itself as a really separate race and will have an intense "people consciousness." Its intimate life will be restricted to itself. Clan loyalty or people loyalty will be the highest virtue. If becoming a Christian offends this clan loyalty, if it means 'leaving my people and joining some other people' then the growth of the Church will be very slow. Whether persons of other tribes or castes become Christians or Communists makes little difference to persons of intense people consciousness. What counts is "what our people are doing." Thus it happens that Christianity, as long as it remains outside a people, makes very slow progress, but, once inside, it flows readily throughout it.

Let us imagine a cupboard full of trays, each one filled with a sterile medium like broth. If bacteria should land in some one tray, they would spread across it far more rapidly than they would go to the next tray up or down. The cupboard is a country. The trays are its separate peoples. The bacteria—beneficent we trust—are congregations. If we do not make this illustration go on all fours, it will yield understanding of the way in which Christianity flows throughout a people more readily than it passes from one to another.

Missions in general coming from a homogeneous society in the West have failed to recognize the separateness of peoples, their vivid self consciousness, and the high significance of that people "in which a Christward movement has been born." The entire methodology of church growth used by missionaries and nationals trained by them is patterned after pietistic church growth in the Protestant West during the last two centuries. That is to say, it is church growth within a nominally Christian land where people consciousness is at a minimum. The convert in the West has acute consciousness of personal ethical and religious advance, but none of traitorously leaving his race. In conversion he leaves a few, but joins more and better members of his own folk. Mission procedures have been geared to this kind of conversion out of a previously Christianized population. Whereas amongst the peoples which constitute so much of the non-Occidental nations, so frequently the convert, together with a consciousness of personal religious advance, feels that he is basely leaving his race. How to get conversions and church growth without inducing that traitorous feeling in each convert is a central problem which churches must solve if they are to grow.

In this book we shall see six cases, in each of which mission procedures have impinged on people consciousness and crossed swords with people loyalties in different ways to produce different degrees of church growth. These six histories are presented both to throw light on how

Churches do and do not grow, and to make available some of the evidence out of which a people movement philosophy and methodology of missions has emerged. Facts are presented. These were gathered on the spot in the areas visited. Conferences with mission staffs, Indian and non-Indian, and with church members aided our understanding of the present position and the process by which it evolved. Larger conferences in which leaders from many stations assembled, enabled us to supplement the information gathered from field study and to test our first tentative conclusions by submitting them to the judgment of Christian men and women from a wide territory surrounding the areas we had visited.

The people movement point of view is nothing descending ready made from the sky. It has different meanings in different peoples and under different circumstances. While there are general principles which are applicable to most peoples, there are also specific differences which keep people movements in Africa from being exactly like those in Formosa, and group movements from within the Karens from being exactly like those from within the Kabiris. Further evidence needs to be compiled. Some of the light in the succeeding pages may need to be corrected. Should there be any who dissent from these conclusions as to how the Churches grow, we cordially invite him to investigate cases of 200% and of 12% per decade church growth and to share his conclusions as to what produces each type of growth. Missions need the truth as to what makes for sound and great church growth. All serious studies whether they confirm, correct, or extend these findings are valuable additions to the science of missions.

II

GROUP CONVERSION

A. L. Warnshuis

THERE is a real difference between evangelism in a Christian environment and Christian missions to people of another religion. That difference arises from the fact that in one case the aim is a revival of religion, calling upon individuals to an awakening of faith, to deeper devotion, to higher ethical living, to greater loyalty. Here there is no separation of the individual from the society in which he lives or from the religion of the community. In going to other lands the missionary aims at bringing the Christian gospel to people of another faith. Many of them may be highly religious, and the missionary's task is not that of reviving their faith or deepening their devotion. Thus the missionary is confronted with the question of the relation of Christianity to other living religions—a question that the evangelist in a Christian community does not face.

Another difference is that which arises from the individualistic character of Western civilization. Western individualism is a modern development. With the rise of industrialism, the growth of great cities and the increasing ease of transportation, our social life has been atomized. Family and group relationships are broken up. The missionary more or less unconsciously thinks of these social conditions as normal. As he goes to other lands, he has not fully understood that the communal principle still

dominates social relationships there. True, the spread of
Western industrialism is beginning to have the same effect
in Asia and Africa as in the West. This is one of the forces
that tend to break down the family worship of Confucian-
ism. The gold mines of Johannesburg and the copper
mines of Central Africa are destroying tribal religion
in Africa. However, eighty per cent of the population in
Asia and Africa still live in rural villages, where comn inal
loyalty is insistently demanded. Disloyalty to the group
is a capital crime in Africa. For murder the criminal
may make atonement by the payment of a fine. For disloyalty to the clan or tribe, which is treason, there can
be no atonement and the penalty must necessarily be
banishment or death. The missionary seeking to win
individuals, separating the converts from their social
groups, seems to be preaching treason, while an evangelist
in a Christian community in his work for individuals will
be a patriot helping men to be better citizens.

When these differences are recognized, it is easy to see
why conversion by groups is natural and necessary.
Religion is a community interest and concern and e ich
group of mankind has its own religion to which the members conform because they belong to a particu'ar tribe
or nation. Privately, perhaps one may believe as he likes,
but outwardly he must conform or be condemned as a
traitor. The demand of modern states to control the religion of their people is evidence of this fact of social life,
as well as a recognition of the power of religion in the life
and purposes of people. Minority religious groups have
usually faced persecution and have succeeded, at best, in
winning a grudging tolerance. So netimes, to be sure,
more than one faith has existed in a given community,

as in Japan and China, but only when each religion has
been partially assimilated by the other and accorded community support. It is in this connection that the recent
official recognition of Christianity as one of the religions
of Japan should be studied to understand the significance
of that action. In Moslem lands, Christianity has survived as the faith of a minority only where that minority
had a community consciousness and was granted recognition. So in the Roman Empire persecution of Christians ceased when their religion was made a community
affair. At first Christianity became only one of the state
religions. Later, when it became the only recognized faith,
other faiths and unorthodox forms of Christianity were
persecuted.

When Christianity becomes the faith of a community,
before long a certain tension arises between the Christian
conscience and the standards of the community's life. So,
in the fourth century, when Christianity was accepted by
the Roman Empire as the community faith, the tension expressed itself in the rise of monasticism. The monks
protested against the compromises of the Christian ethical
standards in the community religion which passed for
Christianity and withdrew from the community to
dwell apart or to establish communities of their own where
they could attain more nearly to what they regarded as
Christian ideals. Through the centuries there have been
many movements among Christian peoples for the enforc-
ing of higher standards—never more than in the nineteenth
and twentieth centuries. These are evidences of the
vitality of Christianity. In this way the fuller meaning
and power of the Christian faith are developed after it
has once been adopted by the community as a whole

These revivals within the community religion should be differentiated from missionary propagation of religion into another community.

History adds its testimony to this truth. The propagation of religion from one community or land to another has never been accomplished by detaching individuals from their social groupings. Men never do anything of importance except in groups, and religion has been propagated only by group movements. It is true that the appeal of Jesus was largely to individuals. But these were strictly within the one people, and of them none was ostracised for becoming His disciple. Indeed, since our Lord presented the Gospel as the fulfilment of the religion of Israel, it seems reasonable to suppose that most disciples whom we know as individuals, represented family groups which accepted Jesus as Messiah. When the Church started to grow on the day of Pentecost, 3000 were added in one day. A little later the men alone numbered 5000. Multitudes both of men and women were again and again added to the Lord. A great company of the priests were obedient to the faith. The whole of two villages, Lydda and Sharon, came to Christ on a single day. In Paul's journeys while he often spoke to individuals, the churches without exception arose when a segment of a community moved rapidly into the Christian faith. The expansion of Christendom in Europe has proceeded only as it was adopted as the group faith of the communities that accepted it. These historical facts are well summarized in the following quotations from Professor Latourette's book, *The Unquenchable Light*:

In the early centuries (p. 15), "As time passed, entire communities began to enter the churches and Christianity

tended to become a group affair. It was thus that the
conversion of the Roman Empire was completed. The
process had begun before Constantine. In about thirty years
as a bishop in Pontus, Gregory Thaumaturgos is said to
have witnessed the accession to the Church of the vast
majority in the territory covered by his see. Beginning
with Constantine, because of the favor of the Emperors,
the movement was accelerated. The success of Martin
of Tours in the fourth century was probably paralleled in
many another diocese. One of the most notable of the
group conversions was that accomplished in the Kingdom
of Armenia, on the eastern borders of the Roman Empire.
That event is so shrouded in legend that we cannot obtain
a clear knowledge of the details or ascertain the motives.
It seems well established, however, that, led by the king
and the nobility, within the span of a few years the entire
nation adopted Christianity. The shrines and the endow-
ments of the pre-Christian cult seem to have been trans-
ferred to the new faith. Under such circumstances the
life and teachings of Jesus could have been only a minor
factor in the adoption of Christianity for the multitude
could have known little about them. Even many of the
priests could have only the most superficial acquaintance
with them. It was not until several generations after the
formal conversion that through the translation and preparation of literature and through contact with the older
Christianity in the Roman Empire an appreciation of the
meaning of Jesus grew and deepened."

In the Middle Ages (p. 47). "The initiative of monarchs and princes was fully as important as in the preceding period. It was usually these, the natural leaders,
through whom acceptance of the faith was accomplished.

Some of the rulers seem to have been actuated by a genuine, even if not always understanding zeal for the Christian faith. Some of them appear also to have been moved by political considerations. It seems fairly clear, for example, that Olaf Tryggvason and Olaf Heraldsson, the kings who were largely responsible for the conversion of Norway, used their advocacy of the faith to build up the royal power against the nobles. The latter had as part of their perquisite the control of the local pagan shrines. By abolishing paganism the Olafs would reduce the functions of the chieftains and enhance their own authority. So, too, Kings Geisa and Stephen of Hungary carried on simultaneously the conversion of the Magyars and the welding of them into a unified monarchy. Presumably the resistance of members of the old nobility was as much due to dislike for the curtailment of their position by the new political order as it was to hatred for the new faith. In Poland under Boleslaw Chrobry the extension of royal power and of territory went hand in hand with the spread of the faith and presumably the pagan reaction which followed Boleslaw's death was directed against Christianity as a bulwark of the innovating political order.

"Imperialism was one of the chief agencies for the propagation of Christianity among the Slavs on the German borders. Even more than in the preceding period the Germans backed with force their efforts at conversion. From the time of Henry E. Fowler and Otto I, strong German monarchs used baptism and the furtherance of an ecclesiastical establishment to extend their rule over the Wends on their northern marches. The Wends fiercely and stubbornly resisted, and the final triumph of Christianity was accomplished more through colonization by Germans and the extermination or assimilation of the Wends than by the voluntary acceptance of Baptism. The exploits of the Knights of the Sword and the Teutonic Knights in subjugating to German power and German Christianity and culture the peoples on the Baltic south of the Gulf of Finland are one of the commonplaces of medieval history.

"The Association of Christianity with imperialism was not confined to the Germans. The spread of Christianity in Finland was a phase of the Swedish conquest. For a time, German imperialism and mission clashed on the Baltic with the more weakly supported Danish commercial, political and ecclesiastical ambition. The first successful missionary efforts among the Pomeranians were at the initiative of a Polish ruler who wished in this fashion to extend his domains."

As we read this history, these mass conversions, judged from their effect upon individuals or on one or two generations, seem often to have been tragic failures, but judged from the influence upon the community they were nothing less than the conversion of Europe. Repudiating the use of force, and relying upon the persuasive influence of teaching and example, we should recognize the fact that it is by the conversion of communities that religion is propagated across the boundary lines of races and cultures. The conversion of a group may not immediately mean much in the achievement of a Christian way of life, but it does mean that the group or community has turned toward The Way, and the direction of its purpose is set toward a Christian goal.

Professor John Foster in his book, *Then and Now* (p. 134), tells of a group of missionaries and ex-missionaries who were studying mass movements. One of the group, however, was a professor of the Old Testament, with no personal missionary experience. When somebody expressed a doubt as to whether he was interested in this discussion, the professor looked up with a smile and said: "You know the whole of my subject might be described under the title, 'How a mass movement became the Church' or 'From the tribes of Egypt to the Ecclesia of God.' That is what the Old Testament is about."

In recent years, this principle of group conversion has been increasingly recognized in India, by some missions in Africa and in the Netherlands Indies. For example, in central Celebes, one finds some of the most significant Christian missionary work of modern times. The two Dutch missionaries, who began their work there in 1890, sought first of all to learn the customs of the people and to become identified with them in thought and speech. They refused to baptize individual converts and resolutely waited until the people were ready to come as families and as village groups. After eighteen years of ground work in 1908 they baptized the first group of 180, and thus prepared the way for other groups, who came not in great masses but as sociological units acting upon their own convictions. Today 34 years later the Christian Church among the people numbers more than 45,000, and—if missionary work can proceed normally—the time is not far distant when the whole population of central Celebes will be Christianized. These tribesmen are making the transition to Christianity without any cataclysmic break with their past. Christianity in no sense has destroyed their culture, but has served to purify, to enrich and to preserve it.

The motives which underlie group movements are often questioned. Where or when are motives not mixed? The Apostle Paul found in Rome that envy and strife were mingled with good will in the preaching of Christ. A whole chapter in Dr. J. W. Pickett's thoroughgoing study, *Christian Mass Movements in India*, is given to a critical study of motives, of which forty instances are given. The remarkable conclusion is that the motives which lead people to Christ in people movements are those that lead individuals anywhere to Him. The sick with divers diseases came to Jesus and He healed them. Social, political and economic conditions are not to be wholly separated from religion in Asia and Africa any more than in America and Europe. This does not mean that right relationships are not to be emphasized between that which is fundamental and primary and that which is secondary and inconsequential. The consciousness of urgent need is almost a necessary prerequisite to the acceptance of the gospel message, even though it may not be possible to speak of the need as arising from a "sense of sin." Among the self-satisfied and complacent the gospel rarely receives a hearing. What leads people to come to the preacher is not nearly so important as that the preacher should seize the opportunity to teach them. Doctor Wasson, in his recent book, *Church Growth in Korea*, writes of the environmental factors, but then he emphasizes the fact that these factors were only allies, and the growth of the Church depended upon its teaching and the way in which the Church related itself to the life problems of its members. The real problem is not how group movements begin but what to do with them when they come.

Closely associated with the question of motives is that other question of how much knowledge should be required of new converts before admitting them into the Church. A well-known missionary writes in a recent letter as follows:

"One of the strong points of Islam in its rapid expansion has been the brevity of its creed 'There is no God but God, and Mohammed is the Prophet of God.' Both practically and legally this is all that is required. Is it not possible for Christian converts to begin with something definite, simple and short?"

May our answer not be that the Apostle Paul's creed was even shorter—Jesus is Lord? Nobody would suggest the admission of an untaught multitude to merely nominal membership of the Church. There will be minimum requirements before baptizing. But the emphasis should be on the teaching of the converts after their admission into the Church. Jesus said, "Make disciples." He did not say, "Make Christians." Too often our teaching efforts are devoted to the enquirer and he finishes his schooling when he is baptized. After that his further education often depends upon his own initiative. Baptism should mark not graduation from school but the beginning of learning. Canon Barry has written:

"The chief concern of self-centered societies is the safeguarding of their own frontiers......The chief concern of the Christian society, at least when it is true to its own character, is to be going out into the highways and gathering in both 'bad and good.' It is not a society of select persons, but the home and school both of saints and sinners." (*The Relevance of the Church, p.* 67.)

To a large extent, all religious work is with individuals. In group conversion, the individual is still as important as ever. Groups are influenced through individuals. The mistake occurs when the objective is only the individual who is separated from the group. Instead of separating him from the group, the individual should lead the way into the group. The fact cannot be questioned that many noble examples of strong Christian faith and of devoted living have been produced by work for separate individuals. This is especially true of converts directly from other religions. The tragic story of the third and fourth generations of children of such converts is not often told. Torn away from their social group ostracized by their relatives, detached from their environment and not numerous enough to form a new group of any consequence, these individuals have tended often to imitate the popular vices. Moral lapses not infrequently occur among them unless the church group has been able to provide the training that is needed. On the whole, the record of individual converts shows no higher level of achievements in character than of those who came as groups. In a group movement, the individuals aid each other in growing in grace and knowledge. The Church in the New Testament epistles is a brotherhood.

For the expansion of the Christian Church the witness of an individual, however good, in a group-conscious community is not equal to the testimony of the group, because of the suspicion of the unrelated, discredited individual. The evidence of the value of the testimony of the group is clearly seen in a convincing way in the experience in Southern India, where groups from the Sudra castes are now coming into the Church in considerable numbers because of redemption seen in Depressed Caste churches.

This principle of group conversion ought to be the fundamental principle of missionary work everywhere, including also that among the American Indians. It should affect the training of missionaries who, in addition to all the preparation needed for work in this country, should be given some help in determining their attitude toward men of other faiths and in understanding a communal society. To send out young missionaries, fresh from the schools that are intended primarily for the training of workers in a Christian community, without any special knowledge of anthropology, sociology and non-Christian religions[1], is a practice that is no longer excusable. So, too, the training of the pastors and preachers in the younger Churches must no longer be patterned on that given in the West for young men going to be ministers in Jonesville. Such training must be adapted to the needs of the community whom these men are to serve. These men, taught to appreciate the true values in the religious and social life of their home community will then strive to purify and enrich that life by bringing to it the grace and power of Jesus Christ. Moreover, men and women missionaries of church and school and hospital will not be concerned only with separate individuals in scores of families but will be united in planning and working to reach the whole family of those individuals with whom they may be in contact.

Briefly summarized, the wrong way to try to build up the Church in a non-Christian land is by the conversion of individuals extracted from dozens of different families, clans, villages and social groups. Such converts are prompt-

---

(1) And more particularly without any knowledge of group conversion.

ly ostracized, separated from their relations and cut off from their roots in the past of their own peoples. Such a church is only a conglomeration of individuals—often held together only by the cement of foreign money. That kind of church has no community interest nor any influence in the community and continues indefinitely dependent upon missionary aid.

The better way is by recognition of the principle that the Church grows along racial lines in social strata. The right and natural growth of the Church is by the conversion of groups, where Christian forces help some group reconstruct its life, individual and corporate, around Jesus Christ.

III

THE GARA REVIVAL

J. W. PICKETT

THE Garas are a numerous oppressed class people living in a territory extending from eastern Madhya Pradesh to the Bay of Bengal. The center of population lies in Orissa. In Madhya Pradesh the Garas are a scattered caste living in small groups of one to ten families. In Orissa they are the principal oppressed caste and live in groups of from five to seventy-five houses. There is a tradition to the effect that at one time they were the ruling race in all, or at least a central part, of this territory, but with the incoming of the upper castes have been degraded to the untouchable position they now occupy. They are addicted to drink and eat the flesh of animals found dead. One landlord said to us while he was sitting in a Church in the Christian section of the village, "Before these people became Christians we never came into this part of the village. If we wanted anyone for work, we would stand outside the group of huts and call for him." These people are musical. Usually a part of their livelihood is earned by playing musical instruments and dancing at weddings, festivals and the like. Where they comprise a large proportion of the population, they are also weavers, cultivators and village menials.

This is the people then in the midst of which an active Christian movement is found. It began in the English

Baptist mission field of Sambhalpur about 1900 and spread west into Raigarh. In 1910 the Mission of the Evangelical Synod of North America took over the Raigarh territory and with it a few Baptist families. For 12 years the territory was worked from Sakti, thirty miles to the west, but the results were unsatisfactory The increase was disappointing. In 1922 the Rev. Y. Prakash determined to live in the territory itself and established himself at Charpali, a small interior village where there were then a total of 21 Christians. At first he did not learn the Ooriya language and had a number of Hindi-speaking assistants of non-Gara origin. He made small headway, even though his residence was among the people. By 1927 he had learned Ooriya, learned the ways of the people and began using Gara convert assistants. The number of conversions rose sharply and has continued steadily. The establishment of a mission station at Chandrapur, with Mr. Albrecht in charge, has materially strengthened the work.

At the present time there are in the neighborhood of 1000 Christians. Over 100 were baptized in the week prior to our survey of the field. There are 30 paid workers and the total budget for this area worked by Mr. Albrecht and Mr. Prakash is about 500 rupees per month. There are sixty villages in which there are Christians. About 25 of these have a worker resident in them. This makes possible a strong programme of instruction and worship. The employment of such a large proportion of the new Christian population, however, while it bespeaks a most commendable interest on the part of the Mission, and does enable a high standard of instruction to be attained, is a procedure fraught with some dangers. The paid staff of 30 should be enough to care for the Church

till it has grown to be one of several thousands. We recommend that this question of the proportion of paid staff
to the total Christian population be made a matter of study,
and that in the meantime no further additions to the paid
staff be made. The problem is partly one as how best to
shift the Church on to a self-supporting basis. It would
be helpful for those in charge to visit and study other
people movement areas such as the Telugu field, and the
Churches established amongst the Garas by the Baptists
and the Mennonites, with this matter of self-support as a
main point of inquiry.

There are a number of sound features of the work
which unquestionably help to spread and deepen this
caste-wise Christian revival. Although Ooriya is not the
official language of Raigarh, it is used by the Christian
Church and its preachers for the simple reason that it is
the language of the Gara people. The Christians learn
the Lord's Prayer, the Creed, their hymns, and the Ten
Commandments in Ooriya. An Ooriya book, "Mukti
Marg," produced by the Baptists and containing a metrical life of Christ and other useful selections, has been influential in building Christian consciousness, and forms an
established part of the course of instruction. The native
Ooriya dances, the Ooriya drums and cymbals and Ooriya
village tunes to which are set various local compositions
have been encouraged. Our visit was the occasion of
two evening dances when a very skilful exhibition of
drumming was given. At Bhukta, a village many miles from
the railway, in the heart of the Christian movement, an
annual mela is held. At this the Christians for miles around
assemble. Thus the Christian religion appears before the
people in Indian costume. People can pay attention to

its message because they are not distracted and misled by
its garb.

An important phase of the Christian movement is that
which centers around the boarding school at Charpali.
From this school have been eliminated all those features
which might alienate the pupils from their people and their
village ways. The school is in a village far off the beaten
track. The dwellings are simple. The teachers as far as
possible are Gara Christians. The children are taught to
regard the spread of the faith amongst their unconverted
Gara relatives as a primary duty. Village musical instruments are kept and skill in their use is inculcated. The
school is an instrument for enlightening and aiding the
Gara Revival. It is a servant of the growing Church.

The use of a simple ritual of worship and the building
of chapels—cheap structures of mud and country tile
or thatch—is a strong feature of the work. The values
of regular daily worship, according to a simple but carefully prepared, year-round out-line, yet remain to be
explored. We recommend that at the first meeting of the
workers careful instruction in, 'how to conduct daily worship' be given; and that through the year a definite attempt
be made to set apart in each village a place for worship,
and to hold a service of worship there each day.

All these features recounted in the paragraphs above,
mean that Christianity is felt by the people to be their own
religion and thus flourishes. We are continually impressed by the degree to which rural group conversion
churches, because of their inevitable and unavoidable
integration with the life of the people, are understood
by the surrounding peoples. Perhaps one element in
the rapid growth of all such churches is that the essential

message of the Church is better understood or is less mis-
understood, than it is in churches which are the result of
"Christianization by extraction." Furthermore the Christians themselves look on their religion not as something
imposed on them from without, something whose true
leaders are the affluent foreigners, not as the adoption of
a foreign religion, but as the adoption of a superior Indian
way to God. Most of the customs and traditions, the
institutions and relationships which make up their lives
are preserved and transformed by this type of Christianization. "What was ours, that, redeemed, remains ours.
Though we are new creatures in Christ Jesus, still we can
recognize ourselves and our neighbors as the very people
who have been redeemed." The leaders of the Church—
untrained though they must be at the beginning of a
movement—are of one piece with the people of the Church.
Christianity becomes not something which a group of
people, largely foreignized and separated from their kind,
is doing but rather a way of life which is going to redeem
an entire people. And in very truth in this rural people
movement, Christianity is the caste's own religion. These
Gara Christians have heard about the new Way from their
own people in their own mother tongue. They have been
instructed in the Christian faith by their own relatives
and friends. Their relations are amongst the leaders of
the Church and they themselves become carriers of the
Word. Thus the people movement moves, and a constantly widening stream of families pours into the Kingdom.

At Seraipali, a conversation with the landlord indicated that the caste people here are getting the same point
of view as the caste people in the Telugu country. They

are now puzzled about the richness of life and the secret power which they observe in Christians and in the Christian community so recently Untouchable. The next step should normally be for one or more castes from amongst them to decide that they want that same richness and power. It may well be that, by an outreaching faith and with the living example in front of them, the process which took so many years in the Telugu country, can be induced in a shorter time in this region and that thus here, too, there will be a series of people movements amongst many castes.

In this region there is a caste of sweepers, known as Ghassiyas, who appear to be quite interested in Christianity. But the Gara converts have not been eager to bring them into the Church. Several of the Ghassiyas indicated to us a desire to learn of Christ and our discussions with Christians both at Seraipali and later on at Bansa and Beltikri left us hopeful that an active and sustained effort by the Missions of Garaland would break down barriers and open the way for a general movement of Ghassiyas to Christ. Such a movement would save the Church from one of the gravest dangers confronting it, and would be for a most down-trodden people a means of escape and of entrance into the abundant life promised by our Lord.

The Ooriya Garas, as has been said, are a populous caste of over 300,000 souls, extending in a south-easterly direction from this territory of the Evangelical Mission some two hundred miles into Orissa. The English Baptist Mission has a flourishing work among them, centering at Balangir. The movement with which the Evangelical Mission is associated, as has been earlier indicated, had its genesis in the work of this Baptist Mission, as did also the work of the General Conference Mennonite Mission to which we shall presently refer. It will be possible to reinforce each of these movements by organizing a Gara Evangelization Council, pooling the resources of experience and understanding accumulated separately and planning a unified poli cy and program for bringing the Garas to Christian faith and purpose.

Of particular importance to this Mission is the fact that there is a great possibility of spreading the existing revival from the Ooriya-speaking Garas to their blood-brothers and close neighbors the Lariya, or Chhattisgarhi-speaking Garas. There are strong indications that this is going to happen in the Basna field. Carrying the Gara revival north and west will bring it into that part of Chhattisgarh which is strongly occupied by the forces of the Evangelical and other missions and may under God be the means of spreading the Faith throughout Chhattisgarh.

The value of the Gara people movement to the Christian work in Chhattisgarh is considerable, and we recommend that careful thought be given to letting the Satnamis, Gonds, Ghassiyas and Lariya Garas throughout Chhatisgarh know about the Gara revival. Possibly a team of Gara singers and drummers could visit the Madku Ghat Mela or make a tour of mission stations, being taken especially to those centers where people are contemplating entering the Christian life. The team should be accompanied by one who can interpret the entire Gara movement to the Chhattisgarhi audiences, tell the thrilling stories of growth through persecution, and assure his listeners that similar people movements can and will take place amongst the Satnamis and other castes. The Evangelical Mission has an instrument here

by which to galvanize its Satnami work into renewed life—
a living, present day, nearby demonstration of the fact that
Jesus Christ redeems whole villages of people who com-
mit their lives into his hand.

Jagdishpur is a station of the General Conference
Mennonite Mission, located near Basna in the Raipur
District. Here exists another overflow of the Baptist
Gara people movement. It started in 1916 through the
efforts of one, Gopal by name, who having been baptized
in Patna State migrated to a village near Basna. He was
determined that his unconverted caste-fellows should hear
the good news, and after unsuccessful attempts to bring
help from Baptists and Evangelicals enlisted the aid of the
Mennonites. He was the moving spirit for several years
and led hundreds to Christ. A converted man in the
midst of his own approachable caste forty miles from
a mission station was again the key to revival.

Ingathering continued till 1923. By that time about
750 people living in 42 villages in a territory ten by fifteen
miles in extent had been baptized. In 1923 the people
movement was arrested. Between 1923 and 1936 while
the Baptist Church was growing from 8,000 to 15,000, the
Mennonite Church of these same Gara people remained
stationary at about 700. The exact figures are as follows:

        1924 .. 746
        1926 .. 807
        1928 .. 850
        1930 .. 652
        1933 .. 675
        1935 .. 703

The causes leading to the arrest of this movement
are so evident and so instructive for all Christians con-

cerned in caste-wise revivals that we relate them, not to
assess blame, but to illuminate the process by which
Churches grow and decline.

At the outset, as was but natural at that time, there
was an almost total lack of understanding of how the
Church in India has grown, i.e. of how people movements
have been developed into vigorous Churches. In the
reports of 1924-34 there is no reference whatever to the
fact that all the growth had taken place in one caste.
Garas are mentioned, but not as the great open door, not
as any more hopeful than the Gonds or the Aghariyas. No
enumeration of the unconverted Garas was attempted.
Indeed, because of the problems which the Gara converts
brought with them into the Church, there was some tendency to regard these people as peculiarly difficult, and to
question the value of more Garas in the Church. An able
and vigorous evangelistic program was carried out but
on an inter-caste basis. The unit to be approached was
the village, not a given caste. The sociological organism
of the tribe or caste was believed to be of little importance
in the jungle territory around Basna, a mistake often made
by missions. Church evangelistic campaigns sent Christians out to witness to all alike, rather than to the unconverted amongst their own relatives and former caste-fellows.
To sum it up, the open door was not recognized, and the
Christian forces flung themselves against the granite walls.

The second cause for stoppage was the sudden change
of regime. In the beginning the Mission policy was one of
granting generous privileges to Christians, of treating the
new Christians in the same way as the older central station
communities. Liberal aids to the education of the children
and economic assistance of various sorts seemed reasonable.

At the time of baptism a new *sari* or *dhoti* or a few annas were given to the convert. This policy was definitely altered in 1924 and many privileges were cut off. A goal was attempted which made for self-confidence and initiative. No transportation of children going to boarding school at Janjgir 60 miles away and at Mohidih 32 miles away was given. The pupils walked to and fro. No Christmas gifts were given to employees. The change from the one basis to the other basis is always difficult. In Basna it helped to stop growth.

Again, when a station was established at Jagdishpur in 1924, a large building program was necessary. Abundant work was provided for Christians. Poorer Christians moved to Jagdishpur and settled there. Although the larger number of the Christian community stayed in the villages and was not directly affected by this building program, nevertheless when, in addition to the changes indicated in the foregoing paragraphs, building work also ceased, Christians living in or near Jagdishpur tended to feel themselves ill-treated, and the pressure fell upon the missionaries, who, despite a policy which leaned the other way, felt that they really ought to do something to lift the economic status of the Christian community. A village school and dispensary were started. A "Weavers' Association" was formed (these Garas are weavers by trade) to buy yarn and sell cloth co-operatively. This took a considerable share of time and attention. Jagdishpur and the nearby villages became a typical mission station with the bulk of the effort being inevitably spent on the Christian community. This care (medical, educational, and economic) tended to transform the Christians into people who considered themselves the beneficiaries of the Mission and to transform the Mission into an organization which considered its primary function that of caring for Christians. That this transformation did not become complete was due in part to the evangelistic zeal of the missionaries, in part to a recognition of the danger and in part to the fact that the metamorphosis had not gone on for a sufficient length of time.

But while ingathering had ceased owing to the above-mentioned causes, two valuable aspects of Church building were being emphasized. Of these the first was the development of a trained lay leadership. Many of the Christian villages have a Christian "mukhtiyar," who conducts worship and heads the local panchayat or council. He gives his services free. At the time of our survey, several of these lay leaders walked in some distance and gave a couple of days of time to attend our meetings and help in the work. The tradition has been established in these 25 villages that the service of God and the Church is a privilege, not a source of income. This tradition should be sedulously cultivated in the years ahead. It will be invaluable as expansion takes place.

The second element of marked strength is the thorough course in the Bible. The local missionaries believe in the Bible and believe in teaching the Bible. Mr. Moyer has worked out careful courses of instruction, skilfully reinforced with abundant pictures. These courses are both for Christians, and, what is more unusual, for non-Christians hearing the Gospel for the first time. The workers and the lay leaders are "Bible Preachers" who teach the Word of God with painstaking care. As this is continued during the coming period of growth, it will do much toward building a large, vital Church firmly based on enduring Scriptural foundations.

We believe that this teaching program will gain in effectiveness as it is linked with a program of regular worship, which should be daily worship if possible. Lay leaders will need careful training to enable them to carry this on. The building, as far as possible by the villagers themselves, of simple chapels is highly desirable. Many missions undertake to supply the roof, if the people provide the land, walls, windows and doors. Where a chapel is not immediately feasible, an outdoor but fenced worship plat-form (*chabutra*) can be built. We recommend that Christian leaders in the near future make a consistent effort to turn the existing body of Christians into churches which worship regularly and in accordance with a simple liturgy.

During the months just preceding our visit, considera-tion of the lessons of the people movement study led to a concentration of evangelistic effort on groups of people in the two branches of the Gara caste, and in the Gond tribe. The response has been encouraging. New Ooriya Garas and a number of Chhattisgarhi Garas (the Hindi-speaking sub-caste not previously reached) have been baptized and others have confessed their faith and requested baptism. A view of the possibilities thus opened up is afforded by the following facts. A census of Garas carried out by the Mission reveals that in the Basna station territory there are probably, 12,000 unconverted Garas. To the east in Raigarh, revival is on amongst the Garas. To the south there are seventy-five Baptist Churches from amongst the Garas. In the territory under consideration, there is a well-established Gara Christian Community of over seven hundred, amply served by able men and women. We urge that primary attention in the days ahead be given to htese 12,000 unconverted Garas. Here lies an obvious

hope of ingathering. Here is the most immediately
approachable. Here are the blood relationships of the
existing Christians. Here is the most widely open door
before the Mennonite Mission.

However there are other peoples which are appealing
and instructive. Near Basna are the Ramramiyas. We
visited several of their villages. They are a remarkable
people who represent a forceful religious movement
which has caught on with the Depressed Classes (chiefly
the Chamars) in a territory forty miles long by ten miles
wide, and is zealously served by them without any outside
financial aid. The adherents of this people movement to
Hinduism believe in Ram as the incarnation of God. All
tattoo the word Ram on their foreheads, some tattoo it
all over their faces and hands, extremists cover every
square inch of their body with the name. They write it
on their clothes and houses. Their religious services
consist of a stamping dance where men and women with
bells on their feet and tall peacock feather "crowns" on
their heads assemble to sing a single refrain for hours,
with various individuals, as the spirit moves them, throw-
ing in a variety of metrical statements in praise of Ram.
Starting some forty years ago with a single man, Parsu,
the movement now numbers about 33,000. Our general
impression was that these people are not unusually approachable—at at least present. The emotional satis-
factions of the peacock feather camp meeting are too
colourful.

Nevertheless the movement does have significance for
Christians. First should be noted the fact that here is a
vigorous religious movement going on without a penny
of foreign financial aid. There is abundant leadership,

plenty of local support, ample dedication of life, and an enthusiasm and a zeal that is contagious. This is an accomplishment of despised Chamars working alone. That the movement is dedicated to the establishment of caste and idol worship, and does not meet the deepest needs of its devotees, should not blind us to the fact that it demonstrates in a vivid way the natural resources at the call of any religious movement which captures the hearts of the people. Christian people movements can and should count on great natural resources, enlarged by the indwelling of the Holy Spirit. Foreign funds and personnel should be used chiefly to guide and direct the awakened people.

Second, despite the apparent unapproachability of the Ramramiyas in the villages visited by us, there are evidences that the movement itself, through its extravagances, its monotony, its immorality, and its inevitable bondage to caste may break up at any time. Certain villages are reported to be on the verge of Christian decision. Certain leaders are said to be greatly dissatisfied with their faith. The impact of the revolt of the Adi-Hindus against Hinduism is certain to tell heavily on these people now apparently so bent on lifting themselves by rivetting on their hands and feet the chains of caste. With the living example of how they have turned to peacock feather crowns, it is likely that they will be particularly friendly to the idea of turning by groups to the enduring crown of righteousness, equality, and spiritual power offered by Christ. We recommend therefore a continuous preaching of the Gospel along people movement lines to these people. The spread of a vital Gara revival into the Ramramiya field from nearby territories may be the key to the situation.

Another attractive people is found in the Satnamis, amongst which the Mennonite Mission is working. A full statement of the Satnami situation will be found in the report on the Evangelical field. Here it will be sufficient to say that the Satnamis are the most numerous approachable caste in Chhattisgarh. It seems inevitable that group ingathering of major proportions will occur from this caste. We are inclined to believe that when it begins, it will come as a flood; and that it is more likely to begin where the message comes as a new story, or where other group ingatherings have demonstrated the people movement pattern. Consequently, while the Satnamis in the villages we visited did not seem unusually approachable, and in common with Satnamis everywhere have suffered from wrong marginal learnings, we believe that the maintenance of work amongst them, and the continued preaching of the Gospel, as a way by which *groups of men, maintaining their social integration* may obtain release from sin and find abundant life, is vitally important.

We would particularly recommend that groups of Satnamis living near villages where Garas have become Christians be made the object of intercession and special effort. During the last ten years there have been only two group movements amongst the Satnamis. Of these the more important is that occurring thirty miles from the Basna revival amongst the Garas and unquestionably influenced by it. Another example of the same thing occurred when a Satnami said to us, "I have an uncle. He writes me saying, 'All the Garas here are becoming Christians, and we Satnamis also wish to become Christians.'" Whether through the Garas or independently, there will arise a great Church from amongst the Satnamis.

IV

THE MANDALA MISSION FIELD

Donald McGavran

IT will be recalled that the purpose of the Mid-India Survey was to discover what growth had taken place along group lines and what possibilities existed of further such growth. The questions asked were: In the midst of awakening peoples on every hand what hope has a given mission of leading one or more to Christ? As peoples grope for light, what can the mission concerned do to bring them into the Church? The work has been to describe those factors which have militated against the normal development of the Church (*i.e.* against people wise ingathering) and to judge, partly from past conversions and partly from present tendencies, which are now the "approachable peoples" from amongst which growth may be expected if vigorous people-wise evangelism is employed.

Mandala was visited with the expectation that here would be found one of the most important cases of arrested people movements. The question was: what should be done in Mandala to reinduce ingathering from amongst the approachable peoples of that great forest district.

History of the Christian Movement in Mandala.

In 1841 six German missionaries were sent out by Pastor Gossner of Berlin in response to an appeal by Sir Donald MacLeod of Jabalpur. They arrived in Mandala in February of 1842 and, of the six, four died there six months later. The others left this part of the country.

In 1885 the field was again occupied, this time by the Church Missionary Society. By 1890 there were in Mandala District six missionaries, four Indian evangelists, and four Indian teachers. In the Indian Christian community were 48 men, 22 women, 39 children, a total of 104. Of these 104, one may assume that about 75 were local converts and about 30 were Christian workers and their families, i. e., people from outside the area. Throughout these early years the similarity of the Mandala Highlands to the Chhota Nagpur Highlands, of the Gonds to the Uraons and Mundas, and of the Mission started by Gossner's missionaries in Chhota Nagpur about 1842 to the Mission started by Gossner's missionaries in Mandala in 1842, impressed itself on the C. M. S. Many of the early workers were Chhota Nagpur Christians of the S. P. G. Mission. It was expected that the great ingatherings in Chhota Nagpur could be reproduced in Mandala. This wise thought may have come close to achievement.

From 1890 to 1897 the numbers of adult baptisms rose steadily, especially around Marpha and Sukulpura. The number of villages in which there were converts increased year by year. A number of families came into the Church from each of these castes—Baiga, Dhulia, Panka and Gond. Of these, probably the Panka converts were the most numerous. The Christian religion was spreading from family to family. The Christian forces do not seem to have been keenly aware of the importance of this people-wise growth, and one sees few, if any, references to the caste of the converts. One of the older workers, a man from Chhota Nagpur said to us, "If in those early days we had recognized the importance of the spread along caste lines, and had worked for the salvation of one caste first, we would have done better."

From 1898 to 1902 also, numbers increased; but the increase was largely achieved through baptisms in the orphanage at Patpara. During these famine years the mission turned to relief work, and large sums of money were given to keep people from starving. From conversations with workers of that period and statements in the Annual Reports, it appears likely that the famine stopped whatever group movements were going on.

The stoppage seems to have had several causes. In the first place, Christians and others were helped financially in the famine years. The impression got abroad both among the Christians and among the non-Christians that the Mission was the "ma-bap," the great provider, only those in dire need of help became Christians, and it was the first duty of the Mission to look after the physical welfare of its converts. With the building of mission stations a great deal of work was provided, cutting and hauling timber, making bricks, building walls, cutting grass for the thatch and so forth. Hard times come frequently in Mandala, and it seemed necessary to make work for the Christians. Sometimes as many as a hundred and fifty out of the two hundred and fifty Christians around Sukulpura and Marpha were being given work to help them eke out a livelihood. The Christians came to believe that when the Mission failed to help them thus, they were being ill-treated—i.e., divorced from their caste and then abandoned by the Mission. The establishment of the large orphanage at Patpara, too, helped to create in the minds of the Christian forces the belief that "Christians must be provided for." When we asked one of the strongest leaders what one thing was needed above all others before the Church could advance in Gondwana he answered, "You must, first of all, make our Christians economically independent, so that other people will look on them as a firmly-established and well-to-do community."

The difficulty of shepherding the scattered Christian community was the second great task. In 1901 there were Christians in 42 villages scattered over the hills and valleys of that forest country. To shepherd these, instruct them, hold divine service with them, and give them Holy Communion, was an onerous task. Missionary after missionary refers to it. Many of these villages had only one or two families living in them. In the 42 villages 16 had only one resident Christian. Either the Christian movement had to gain greater numbers so that groups of at least five to ten families could meet together regularly for worship and instruction, or the movement was headed for stagnation and defeat. Under some specially devoted missionaries these far-flung Christians could be shepherded, but when furloughs occurred, or illness intervened, or the rains descended and the floods came, the farther Christians went without care, despite Herculean efforts to provide it.

It is significant that as far as the records go, no local men were employed as leaders or teachers.

When the difficulty of shepherding, combined with the famine-born paternalism, imported pastors, and other causes, stopped these beginning movements amongst the Pankas, Baigas, Dhulias, and Gonds, the attention of the Mission turned more and more to making provision for

the existent Christians—provision both material and
spiritual. The heavy responsibilities of the orphanage
tended to make the center of the mission at Patpara and
Mandala, whereas the opportunity for ingathering was
at Marpha, 80 miles east. This change did not take place
without a struggle. A series of Annual Reports call attention to the fact that Marpha was being left uncared for,
and plead for adequate forces to staff the eastern field.
Once stopped, caste-wise growth never started again.

A significant set of figures is the following: There
were 1,272 baptisms in the forty-one years 1891-1931.
Of these 958 were in childhood—children of Christians,
or orphans. The remainder, 314 only, represent the total
number of adult converts from the Pankas, Baigas, Gonds,
Dhulias, Kols and other castes. Obviously the numbers
concerned in each caste were very small, not really big
enough to be called a people movement.

Following 1903 it is difficult to trace exactly what
happened. Mr. Hodgkinson, writing 25 years later, states
that in 1901 "fatal rot" set in and decline started. It is
certain that the membership remained approximately
stationary for several years, rising very gradually (with the
baptism of the Patpara orphans?) to 784 in 1913. After
this, numbers decline to 554 in 1921, and back up to 660
in 1935. The period of growth ended with 1903. There
were six and a half hundred then. There are six and a
half hundred now.

The missionaries of sterile Mid-India, like most missionaries in static areas, scorned "mass movements"
and knew little about them. Quite a tale had been
developed about "the large reversions following inju-
dicious and hasty group baptisms in the forests of

Mandala." The facts are that there were neither large group baptisms, nor large reversions. The total reversions number less than a hundred and occurred during a period when baptisms in the orphanage made good the losses, so that at no time was there a significant decline in numbers. The reversions were not clean cut either. Those who "reverted" bore such a relationship to the Church that some years they were counted as Christians and some years they were not. They were carried for years with the hope that with increased shepherding facilities they could be won back into the fold. Though the numbers concerned were small, the importance of the reversions was great. They did not stop ingathering. They merely proved that the Christian movement had been defeated.

A realistic consideration of this field from the point of view of natural growth along caste lines requires that the figures be considered in two blocks. In the first fall the stations of Mandala, Patpara, and Deori. In the second fall Marpha, Sukulpura and the surrounding villages. In the first there have never been any appreciable number of indigenous Christians,—converts who continue to live amongst their people and to follow their ancestral occupation, and who in consequence are able to spread their new found religion amongst their caste fellows. Mandala has always been an urban station with no indigenous Christians in the town or nearby villages. Patpara is a typical institutional mission station, whose principal work through the years has been the orphanage and boarding school. There have been practically no indigenous Christians in the villages nearby. Deori is a Christian land colony typical of the post-famine period in Mid-India. When Deori was first founded there were indigenous Christians in six or eight nearby villages. But with the coming of the Christian colony, these indigenous Christians either were pulled into the central land colony, died out, or moved away. This left Deori as a land settlement of non-typical people, orphanage boys and girls, out of organic connection with the people round about them.

Spiritually all three stations have been sterile. They have not won to Christ groups of men and women in the surrounding villages. This is not attributable to moral depravity or spiritual ignorance. Christians of these stations know the Christian religion, worship the Lord, and live sober and God-fearing lives. It is attributable to the fact that the group is dependent upon the Mission and is out of contact with its neighbours. They have been moulded by the orphanage-mission combination into people so different from their neighbors that they do not and probably cannot mingle with them in an effective way.

In the second block of stations there were many indigenous Christians. Around Marpha and Sukulpura there were two or three hundred men, women, and children (an adult community of a hundred and fifty at the peak) who resided in the villages, out away from the mission stations, in organic contact with their people, knowing of scores of non-Christians relatives, and carrying on their ancestral occupations.

In 1898 the Marpha-Sukulpura field had 202 Christians in it; while the Patpara-Mandala field had 30. In 1936 the proportion is about reversed. In 1898 the vast majority of Christians in this mission were those for whom, because of being in intimate contact with their caste fellows, spiritual reproduction was possible; while in 1936 the vast majority of Christians in this mission are those for whom, because they are in mission settlements, have lost contact with their relatives and are looked on as a different caste of people, spiritual reproduction is, if not impossible, at least very difficult.

The bearing of educational policy on ingathering is to be noted. This Mission has stressed education. Schools were started partly to care for small groups of Christian children in various villages, and partly to bring in converts. In 1917 twelve out of sixteen schools were carried on in villages where there were no Christian children other than the teachers' own. This system endured for many years. The experience here harmonizes with that of other missions. Schools for non-Christians do not lead to the establishment of the Church. Nowhere in Mid-India have we found an instance of ingathering following extensive educational work done amongst non-Christian boys and girls.

Making Sterile Areas Fertile

A sterile area is one in which very slow growth of the Church is taking place largely through the rearing of Christians in orphanages on the one hand, and through the conversion of individuals from various strata on the other hand. In both cases the resulting Christians become members of a loosely integrated community of non-typical people. Growth is very costly. To change a sterile into a fertile area means getting a different type of growth started, growth by natural conversions of adults in some approachable people, adults who remain out in their homes, doing their ancestral tasks, and continuing in organic connection with their non-Christian caste fellows.

It may be taken as axiomatic that in any mission field the hope of church growth lies not in assiduous care of congregations of non-indigenous Christians, but rather in expanding Christian movements in approachable peoples. Applying this general truth to the Mandala field, we may say the only hope of church growth here lies in starting some caste-wise movement.

We may approach the same truth from a different angle. If the loving care of the six hundred Christians of the Mandala district (care which involves not only spiritual oversight of the Church, but also a great deal of material assistance, supervision of land settlements, and employment) is continued, the existing Church may be kept alive indefinitely,—as long, indeed, as funds hold out. With the expenditure of considerable funds, the community might even grow, by excess of births over deaths, to a thousand in the next twenty years.

But since the future of missions holds out little hope that material care can be continued year after year it would seem that before this Church there are but two alternatives; (1), to dwindle with the decrease of foreign funds; (2) to initiate and nurture Christian movements in some approachable caste or castes, thus becoming strongly rooted in the land. Fortunately the Christian community is not completely divorced from the surrounding people. The Christians still know from which caste they have come. A few of them still have relatives, whom they know and visit. This condition will rapidly cease to exist, for as the years pass the Christians who were themselves converts will die, their children will marry the children of Christians, and the Christians will lose organic touch with their former castes. Since every passing year makes divorcement more complete, now is the time to act. For the Christian community the natural door to expansion is the door to the homes of relatives and caste fellows. Every effort should be made to lead the Christians to win their relatives. Every relative won is a means to the winning of others of that caste. "So he went and told his brother, 'We have found the Christ' " is still the most certain way in which the Christian religion is spread.

However, "winning my relatives to Jesus Christ" has a definite and unfortunate connotation for these non-typical, dislocated, orphanage-reared Christians. It means extracting some needy man or woman from his caste and from his village, giving him land or a job in the mission station, usually at mission or missionary expense, educating his children in the mission boarding schools, and making him a part of the non-indigenous Christian group. As long as this picture of what Christianization means dominates the mind of any Christian, he will find it exceedingly difficult to win anyone to Christ, and he will find it almost impossible to start a normal group movement to Christ.

Furthermore 'becoming a Christian' in such sterile areas has a definite and unfortunate connotation for the non-Christian. It means renouncing one's race (caste), leaving one's home, separating forever from one's relatives, marrying into a conglomerate assortment of peoples, and becoming dependent on a kindly but foreign organisation which, of recent years, does not seem quite equal to the job of providing for the existing Christians. As long as this picture dominates the mind, it is difficult for anyone to accept the Saviour and start a people movement to Christ.

On the contrary, where both Christians and non-Christians, know that becoming Christian normally means being baptized with one's family and caste fellows, living on in the same homes, doing the same work, marrying amongst one's own caste people (those who have become Christian), earning one's own livelihood in traditional ways, and within this framework accepting Christ as Lord and Saviour, there the message can be accepted by enough people so that a Church is established, and grows greatly year by year.

Consequently, if the Christian community is going to become evangelistically potent, it should erase from its own mind the picture of a Christianization which divorces converts from the normal life of the district; and should paint in vivid colors on the canvas of its imagination a people movement Christianization. This will not be done merely by exhortations to go out and evangelize. It will be done as leaders get this vision themselves, and place it continually before their people, telling scores of stories illustrating the normal way in which peasants become indigenous Christians; as leaders conduct institutes for lay evangelists, both men and women, where these will be taught in detail how to win their relatives, caste fellows and approachable-caste neighbors; as leaders teach that the ideal is not to extract an individual and unite him to the existing separated Christian community, but is rather to win a whole caste in all the villages of a given valley or district, to have a chapel built by the new Christians in every village, to have pastors from amongst the people themselves, and to let the light of Jesus Christ shine in the hearts of tens of thousands of people in this generation.

Christianization usually starts with the conversion of an individual. With a renewed emphasis on evangelism there should be a number of conversions in the Mandala district in the coming years. If these converts are treated in one way they will become members of the existing Christian community, thus being saved as individuals but lost as potential evangelists to their caste fellows. If the sum total treatment meted out to them, conscious and unconscious, is of another sort they will not only be saved as individuals but will likely start small group movements. As these are properly treated, they may grow to large group movements of, let us say, five hundred adults in from two to ten villages. These in turn should become people movements and vital Christian Churches.

The Mid-India area gives hundreds of instances of individual converts lost as potential evangelists, scores of small movements which were stopped and about a dozen large movements which failed. We have had it borne in upon our consciousness that the most precious gift God gives into the hands of the Christian forces of any area is the individual convert from an approachable caste, who wins his own relatives. He is a pearl of great price. When found, Churches and Missions should give him the best aid available to help him make his small group into a victorious people movement, building a great Christian Church. The task before the C.M.S. is finding such men and with them building the Church in Gondwana.

Finally it will be well to recall that the growth of the Church is the doing of God, not of men. People Movements are dependent on the Holy Spirit, not on any method. Still the Holy Spirit is not a spirit of disorder. As we see the way in which He has led untold thousands

into the Church through group conversions, as we ponder
the fact that the only way in which great church growth
has come to any part of India has been through caste-wise
Christian movements, we are led to believe that the Holy
Spirit desires great ingathering everywhere. It is our
part to find out how He works to increase the Church and
to apply that knowledge to our own field. In a similar
way, the central abiding message of Christian revelation
is that sinful men can be saved through the sacrifice of
Christ. We are resolved to preach but one thing, and that
is Redemption through the Cross. Yet by our preaching
and the on-going life of our mission stations, our non-
Christian brethren are learning "Christianization by extraction," which hardens their hearts against the central message. The clothes in which we dress the central truth must
help people to accept it. Believing fully in the spiritual
nature of our task, and in the pre-eminence of Christ,
this report pleads for a way of presentation which will
permit the redemptive power of the cross to reach every
hamlet and every heart in all Gondwana.

V

AMONG THE BALAHIS

J. W. Pickett

FROM the standpoint of Christian Missions the distinctive feature of Nimar is the responsiveness of people of the Balahi caste to Christianity.

The Balahis are a depressed people upon whom caste has laid a cruel hand. They are labourers, weavers, and village watchmen. Their numbers approach a hundred and fifty thousand. By origin they seem to be an offshoot of the large Kori caste of weavers, one of whose sub-divisions in the United Provinces is the Balahi. It appears that in the Central Provinces they have received accretions from the spinner caste of Katias, themselves probably a branch of the Koris, and from the Mahars, the great menial caste of the Bombay Presidency. The Balahis are reputed to be the oldest residents of Nimar, a belief which accords with the theory that the "Untouchables" of today are descendents of the original inhabitants of the land, who were enslaved by the conquering Aryan immigrants.

Many disabilities are imposed upon the Balahis. They are denied the use of village wells. The temples are closed against them. The village barber will neither shave them nor cut their hair. The tailor will make clothes for them only if he be permitted to take the cloth directly from the merchant, and the washerman will wash for them only if the clothes be brought to the edge of the river or tank and dipped in the water before they are delivered to him. Until recently their children were uniformly excluded from the village schools and even now the right of admission is more theoretical than factual. Not long since they were compelled to wear an earthen spittoon suspended from their necks, lest they defile the ground with their spittle, and a broom hung from their backs to erase the imprint of their feet, lest some caste Hindu walk thereon and be contaminated. Economic exploitation has been as ruthless as social oppression. For the most part they live always in dire poverty chronically under-nourished. Hunger has made them depend for common diet in part upon scraps of food discarded by their neighbours and for feasts upon carcasses of beasts or fowls that disease old age or other cause may have laid down in their way. Poverty has made them welcome the cloth from corpses at the burning ghat.

Worse in its effects than the imposing of social disabilities and economic exploitation has been the concept of Karma by which they have been influenced to regard themselves as a worthless, degraded people. Scars and distortions of personality have resulted from these impacts of Hinduism, but evidence of stern stuff in the Balahi heritage abounds, for they have withstood generations of mistreatment without the loss of potentialities. Masses regard their shame and degradation as inevitable and ordained of God but thousands have responded to the preaching of the Gospel by evincing faith and hope, and in hundreds of homes the Gospel has begun to effect liberation of spirit, reconstruction of personality and transformation of character.

HARDA

In and around Harda few Balahis have been converted and no convert has remained in his village. For some fifty years the Disciples' Mission occupied Harda in force, maintaining a high school, several primary schools, a hostel for Christian boys and a hospital. The boys in the hostel were imported from other districts, alone or with parents who worked for the Mission. Evangelists preached in the villages for a dozen miles or more around Harda, but made no concerted or sustained effort to reach the Balahis. They preached to all castes as they found opportunity and made no effort to concentrate upon the Balahis as an interested caste within which group decisions to follow Christ might be expected. When, in 1929 a program of concentration was necessitated by shortage of finance, the Mission closed its institutions in Harda and withdrew, leaving only one Indian pastor who serves a small congregation from which he receives a small part of his support.

With the new interest in and understanding of people movements, the pastor at Harda has become specially interested in the Balahis. Supported by several educated young men of his congregation he has presented the Gospel to groups of the Balahis in visits to their homes as well as in public preaching. The response has been heartening. Two influential headmen have revealed themselves as having been greatly influenced by Christianity before this approach to them. The father of one of them was for years before his death a secret believer. Entire groups are favorable to Christianity and a deep spiritual hunger seems to be very common within the caste over the entire area.

KHANDWA

Sixty-four miles southwest of Harda, where our study in the Nimar territory began, lies Khandwa, in and around which are thirty-seven hundred Christians associated with the Methodist Episcopal Church. These Christians are nearly, but not quite, all recruited from the Balahi caste. Their accession to Christianity has been wholly typical of the group process which has produced the great Christian populations of Kerala, Tinnevelly, Andhra-Pradesh, Chhota Nagpur, and the Punjab, except for the one feature that they began to turn to Christ as a result of the purposeful concentration upon them selected as a caste which was likely to be responsive to the Gospel.

The history of the work at Khandwa is replete with important lessons. Bishop James M. Thoburn, who was one of the first serious students of people movements in North India, selected the Balahis as a people who would probably hear the Gospel gladly, and advised the ministers under his supervision at Khandwa to work specially for their conversion. Likewise Bishop Thoburn, understanding the disposition of people to act in groups, and recognizing the validity of group action in religion, recommended that the approach be made not to individuals for solitary action but to families and groups of families for joint decision. The movement quickly followed.

We have not been able to procure statistical reports earlier than 1915. The following analysis of records since that time is instructive:

Protestant Christian Community:

1915	.. 1173
1921	.. 3323
1925	.. 2667

1930   .. 2895
1934   .. 3309
1935   .. 3779

An untoward development early in the history of the movement at Khandwa was the coming of the Roman Catholics. On arrival they entered immediately into aggressive competition for the control of the new converts. This has heavily handicapped the effort to build Christian character and experience. Rather than initiate new work of their own even under the favorable conditions resulting from the success of the Methodists, the Roman Catholics have spent their energies in trying to draw Christians away from the Church in which they were converted. The ill effects of their aggression have been most serious in relation to discipline, but have extended to every aspect of congregational and personal life and experience.

Another drag was placed upon progress by the unanticipated effects of famine relief administered in the years 1897-1900 inclusive. The converts learned to expect financial help in times of difficulty, and ministers of the Church, learning to think of themselves as dispensers of charity, lifted from the Church the burdens necessary for the development of its strength.

A third interference with the normal development of the Church has been the acceptance of low standards of expectation, probably imported from the North, concerning the adoption by new converts of Christian ways of life, especially in regard to worship programs and social conventions. Ordinarily worship services have been held only when a salaried man, drawing his support almost entirely from sources outside of the District, was

present. The local Christians have ordinarily participated
in worship only in singing; and so far as we could discover,
their interest in that and other parts of the service has
been half-hearted. The marriage customs of the unconverted Balahis have been followed by the converts, un-
modified except, perhaps, by the elimination of their more
blatantly idolatrous features. Child marriage has not
been appreciably reduced. We were unable to learn of a
single marriage of village Christians by Christian rites
except in families drawing salaries from the Church and
we met one ex-preacher who had recently arranged the
marriage of his minor daughter by non-Christian rites.

Despite these several handicaps the Christian movement has advanced considerably and has to its credit
some very worthwhile achievements. During the year
preceding our visit no fewer than 520 new converts were
baptized, and we found everywhere we went a confident
belief that a new era of numerical advance and qualitative
improvement had begun. We believe that there are solid
grounds for such confidence. The Balahis are waking
up. They will not continue in the state to which Hindu
teaching and oppression have reduced them. They will
not tolerate the continued denial of the implications of
their manhood. There is among them a wisespread recognition that Christianity offers a way of salvation, and that
no other way is open. Among Christians in the district
we found extensive evidence of a desire to improve the
quality of their Christian discipleship. A semi-literate
Christian, converted as a young man thirty years ago
said, "We are just now learning that it is a mistake to be
half-way Christians. We have lost most of what God
offered us because we have not been fully Christian."

The superintendent, the Rev. Salabat Phillip, an experienced Indian minister, evinced acquaintance with the main lessons of our study and eagerness to apply them to the situation within the district.

MANDLESHWAR

Across the border in Central India, fifty miles northwest of Khandwa, is Mandleshwar, a mission station of the United Church of Canada Mission, opened in 1930. A few Balahis were converted in the neighborhood of this town before 1905. Until the station was opened converts were ministered to only through the irregular touring of ministers or lay-missionaries from Indore. At times they saw no minister for more than a year. Their spiritual life suffered and their children grew up with very little Christian knowledge or influence. Some of the children were married to non-Christians and came to count themselves Hindus.

From about 1925 to 1930 there was a slight quickening of interest with a small number of conversions from the Balahis and the Dolis. This led to the establishment in 1930 of a mission station there in charge of the Rev. T. Buchanan. The policy adopted has been the intensive working of the most accessible portion of the field, a strip of territory 10 miles wide and 40 miles long just north of the Narbada river. As a result there has been a steady, though not very large, increase in the Christian community.

Though there were converts from other castes in former years, the active Church now consists very largely of converts from the Balahis. (One of the hopeful aspects of the situation is, however, the movement amongst the

Chamars.) In contrast to those about Khandwa these
have been won, not in entire village groups but one or two
or three families at a time. The community at the time of
our visit numbered 600, of whom 212 were baptised in
1935 and 12 in 1934. Two observations struck us with
great force: first, that the village converts had understood
that the Church did not favor the coming of large groups;
and second, that when it was suggested to them that
group conversions were desirable they agreed heartily
and grew enthusiastic over the possibility of bringing
in large sections of the Balahis and building up the Church
by inducing movements of their people.

There is one way of preaching, accepting and training
converts which limits group action and encourages one
by one conversions. It is usually adopted because it is the
way the missionaries know by their own experience and
training in the West. It is usually defended as the only
sound and careful way. Men say that, unless one is interested in mere numbers, a cautious acceptance of only tested
individuals is necessary. We judge that this has been the
Mandleshwar pattern. It would account for the picture
portrayed in the preceding paragraph.

The work around Mandleshwar shares most of the
characteristics of that about Khandwa. A few marriages
of typical village people have, however, been performed
by Christian rites and the converts examined disclosed a
higher level of knowledge of facts about our Lord and the
creed of the Church. A great door is open around Mandleshwar.

The Balahis are not restricted to the country adjacent
to the three stations on which we have reported. The
Nimar Balahi territory is an irregular rectangle approxi-

mately thirty miles wide and two hundred miles long, extending from the Vindhya rampart on the north to the Satpura mountains on the south and from Hoshangabad and Itarsi on the east to Barwani on the west. This territory is well provided with mission stations. Barwani Tahsil is occupied by the Canadian Presbyterians, Diwas, by the United Church of Northern India affiliated with the United Church of Canada, Mandleshwar by the United Church of Canada, Khandwa and Harsud by the Methodist Episcopal Church, Harda by the Disciples, Banapura, Itarsi and Hoshangabad by the English Friends.

The Balahis are divided among themselves. The largest sub-caste is the Nimarhi. The Christian converts in the Khandwa and Mandleshwar fields are from this sub-caste, which is spread over the whole territory mentioned above. Two other sub-castes are known as Gannora and Katia. Among them no movements toward Christ are known but a sustained effort to win them would probably bring large results.

At present the only active group movements of Balahis to Christ appear to be those around Khandwa and Mandleshwar. However in a number of other regions of the territory mentioned above Balahis are represented in the Church by a larger number of converts than any other caste. We are of the opinion that a concerted movement to bring the Balahis to Christ throughout the entire territory in which they are found in force would be likely to lead large numbers of them to an early confession of Christian faith and discipleship. Whether or not that be the case, we are clear in our conviction that no plan for pushing on with the work will meet the full obligation of the Church if it does not present the call of Christ "Come

unto me" to the whole of the Balahi population throughout the area. We recommend therefore the formation of
a Balahi Evangelization Council that will be charged
with responsibility for developing a united approach to
the Balahis and a united policy and program for winning them to Christ and employing them in the spread
of Christian faith and purpose through the population
as a whole. If this is done and a concerted effort made,
we anticipate the rapid upbuilding of the Christian Church
in this area.

The Evangelization Council would be a voluntary association of those who feel that the great door now open
before them constitutes a call from God to co-operative
work. Its actions would be strictly advisory. Its purpose would be to pool experience, and to help carry fire
from one section of the field to other sections of the field.
At the will of the missions concerned, forces might be lent
from one area to another, to conserve some rapid growth,
or to start the movement where it was quiescent. Tracts
for the Balahis could be published which would be useful
throughout the entire population of 150,000 people.
Summer schools for lay leaders could most readily be
planned and carried through in a united way. Common
standards of expectation would be built up. Common
worship programs and courses of instruction for new
and old Balahi converts would be most economically and
effectively produced by such a Council. While it requires
some imagination to envisage the following development,
we dare to hope that a Balahi Evangelization Council
participated in voluntarily by six Missions and Churches
would normally develop one great Narbada Valley
Church of Christ in this fertile territory. This would be a

Church composed in the beginning of scores of thousands of Christians from the Balahi caste, and then with ever increasing power taking into itself converts from the Chamars, the Dolis, the Mahars, the Mangs, and eventually the caste Hindus.

Because the Vindhya Mountains intervene, the Balahis just described constitute a people geographically distinct from the Balahis of the Malwa plateau and adjacent territories to the north. Limitations of time did not permit a visit in person to the three areas of largest ingathering amongst the plateau Balahis. Conference with the Rev. H. H. Smith, the Rev. D. F. Smith, Miss Clarihue and others, however, indicated that at Ujjain, Kharua, and Sitamau there are village Christian communities of 400, 1000, and 150 from amongst the Balahis. At Sitamau there exists, together with the small Balahi movement, a Chamar movement of 450 persons. At present the Sitamau field seems to be the most active. These three centers are in a straight line, running in a northwesterly direction from Ujjain to Sitamau, a distance of about a hundred and fifty miles, with Kharua in the center. It should be expected that an early development would be the fusing of these three separate areas into one by inducing growth in the intervening country. There are probably 250,000 Balahis north of the Vindhyas, 150,000 of whom live in the territory easily accessible to the United Church of Canada. Since Chamars are in two places associated with Balahis in a movement into the Christian faith, the total Chamar population should probably be added to the Balahi population, thus making an immediately approachable population of at least 300,000. We believe that the Balahis and Chamars north of the Ghats are the great approachable castes of the level plateau land of Malwa, and that in every mission station they are a people who will not merely hear the Gospel but will accept it. The call of the present is a call to evangelize these whom God has prepared to accept the Good News. We therefore recommend that a second Balahi Evangelization Council be formed of those working in the three fruitful areas described above, and that this Council too be charged with making a concerted effort toward the ingathering of these great communities. One of the first duties of the Council when organized will be a careful survey of the situation north of the ghats. A picture even more favorable than that of the Nimar Valley may be disclosed.

VI

POSSIBILITY OF INGATHERING AROUND DHAMTARI

J. W. Pickett

DHAMTARI is the headquarters of a territory occupied by the American Mennonite Mission. Shortly after the establishment of this Mission the famines of 1897-1900 occurred. Hundreds of children were brought to the Mission, which cared for them in orphanages and, later, in other institutions at central stations. Converts have been won, not in groups, but as individuals, and when an individual or a family has been converted, a move to one of the institutional centers of the Mission has seemed normal and proper. Thus the resultant Christian community is collected in Dhamtari and neighboring stations. This Mission is one of the few which has taken a relatively small territory and manned it thoroughly. A comprehensive program of service to the Christian community, and to some extent to the non-Christian public has been carried through with devotion and thoroughness. The Christians have learned to think of themselves as a people apart from the general population and as the beneficiaries of mission expenditures. Although the obligation to witness to Christ has been taught with admirable earnestness, the expectation that converts would not continue to live in their village homes among the non-Christians has heavily handicapped evangelistic efforts. Isolated converts have occasionally been won, but, forsaking their village homes to obtain the benefits of residence in the protected and richly served mission centers, they have forfeited the opportunity to win their fellows to Christ.

These forces might have been overcome and growing churches established in the villages had there been a strong belief in the validity of group conversions. However, as in most missions from the individualistic social order of Western countries, there has been in operation a fear that group movements produce an inferior, if not a purely nominal, brand of Christianity. Two strong rural Churches resulting from group movements have existed within 150 miles of Dhamtari. But, because they were in other provinces and other language areas; and because the missionaries shepherding these churches were English and German, rather than American as the Dhamtari missionaries were, therefore these two significant Christian movements remained practically unknown. Thus though they were both thoroughly Christian, alive, and rapidly growing, Christian leaders at Dhamtari in common with most Christian leaders in Mid-India, distrusted group conversions and preferred the kind of church growth described in the first paragraph. In a similar way neither missionaries nor Indian ministers have been acquainted with the great Churches established by people movements in more distant areas. Thus there has been an inevitable lack of recognition that a normal way for caste-conscious India to come to Christ is through caste-wise revivals.

The total lack anywhere in this Church of groups of village converts appears to be due in part to the fact that the mission plan and organization have not been such as to encourage group conversions. Up to the present time evidence has not been available on which to base the belief, now fortunately growing increasingly common, that one type of organization, planning, expectation, thinking, theory, and work helps to produce the relatively non-reproductive central station churches of mission beneficiaries; while another helps to produce vital, reproductive churches spreading along caste lines. Of course, the establishment of any church means the genuine conversion of men and women, and any genuine conversion is the work of the Holy Spirit, whether that be the conversion of one individual or of many individuals. Thus the close thinking, careful organization, and heavy institutionalism typical of many stations and of this Mennonite Church and Mission would appear to help the Holy Spirit to bring about isolated conversions many of them in boarding schools; whereas another type of thinking and organization would appear to be the medium through which the Holy Spirit works to bring about conversions in natural social units.

The closest example of this second type of thinking and organization lies 100 miles to the east of Dhamtari, where four Baptist missionaries on a relatively small budget are giving guidance and direction to an active people movement among 300,000 Garas. The existing Church in 1936 numbered 12,000 and had 75 practically independent, largely self-supporting congregations. The movement is growing rapidly and in a few decades may well involve the entire caste. Thus it may be said that the Mission with comparatively limited resources, because of following this second type of organization, expectation and method, is helping the entire Gara caste to reconstruct its life around Jesus Christ. One of the most important lessons of this study is that conversion of groups of individuals, contin-

ued residence of converts amongst their fellows, proper
instruction of new converts, adequate use of leaders from
amongst the caste being converted, and many other factors
combine to form a pattern of action which definitely encourages the initiation and growth of people movements.
*One way of Christianization permits and encourages groups of
families from within the same people to come to salvation without
social dislocation in a constant and ever-widening stream. Whereas another way of Christianization permits and encourages individuals of many peoples having been torn from their societies, to
come to salvation in an intermittent and gradually diminishing
trickle.* It is also worthy of note that this coming to faith
in Jesus Christ of families from within one stratum of
society is much more like what happened in the days of
the early Church than is the central station type of Christianization.

We were pleased to discover a growing appreciation
of the group conversion point of view among the missionaries and Indian ministers of the Mennonite Church.
The diagnosis of the existing situation as we have presented
it is not entirely our own but represents the thinking of
those with whom we conferred in Dhamtari.

We believe that a new approach in evangelism has
begun and that the time of ingathering is at hand. Within several castes, groups have been discovered with a very
definite interest in Christianity and hunger for the things
of God. Influential leaders of the Mahar caste have re-
nounced Hinduism and are making encouraging responses
to the presentation of the Gospel. There are large numbers of Satnamis in and near Dhamtari. This is the one
caste from which have come both a large number of individual converts and so in nearby districts several small

arrested people movements. As such it would be presumed to be approachable. Less than one hundred miles to the east of Dhamtari lie areas in which small but vigorous Gara movements are going on. There are Garas in the eastern edge of the Mennonite territory. These unquestionably constitute an approachable group, probably somewhat scattered.

We recommend that all available forces be set at the task of winning groups of these Mahars, Satnamis, Garas, and other possibly accessible castes to Christ, and training them to lead their relations to the Saviour. Work for communities that show no interest in conversion should be closed, if need be, in order that resources may be available for a widespread effort on the above lines. It may be confidently expected that as the Christians seek to overcome the barriers imposed by the individualistic patterns of the past and to win groups to Christ, there will be response. The pearl of great price is a cluster of families who confess faith in Jesus Christ and determine to live the Christian life. These should then receive the best spiritual care available (taking special precautions that financial dependence on the Mission does not develop) and men from amongst them trained for Christian leadership. At the same time the thousands of relatives and near caste-fellows of the converts will certainly become the most approachable people in the entire area—not necessarily the most friendly, though that often is the case, but the most approachable, that is, people from whom decisions for Christ are most likely. Consequently the best men in the Church, foreign or Indian, should be delegated to preach the Word of God amongst these living organic connections of the new Christians.

The place of the existing carefully tended Christian community in the establishment of a Church which will grow is one which deserves the most careful thought. A painstaking analysis of the existing church membership showed that the Christians, coming out of the orphanages and leper asylums, and from the isolated converts brought into the central station from various castes, have a good many relatives throughout the tahsil. There is also a certain degree of visiting between the Christians and their relatives. However, the rich and abundant life made possible by the foreign mission has so lifted the Christian group above its antecedents and racial connections, that no organic relationship remains. The Christians feel no inner drive to evangelize "these who are bone of our bone and flesh of our flesh." The non-Christians on the other hand frankly believe that only those who are willing to desert their caste, chiefly for the richer life made possible through foreign funds, ever become Christians. We speak not in an effort to assess blame, but to state what exists in an attempt to solve the problem of why the existing Church does not spread more rapidly. Perhaps it is served too much.

It is interesting that the allegation so frequently made in regard to people movements, namely that in them persons became Christian from material motives, should be almost universally believed by Hindus in regard to these who have here, and elsewhere, become Christians in a distinctly individualistic fashion. It would seem as if the enriched life has been made possible in such a way as to separate its recipients from their kindred. In this connection, thinking men amongst the Christian community are beginning to realize that this "enriched life"

possible in the Mission Station is an artificial thing, and
that separation of the Christians from their fellows provides
socially and economically only a temporary advantage.
Missions cannot be presumed to remain on forever. The safty
of the community requires integration with the larger group.

The problem involved is the place of the detached
central station Christian community in the kind of evangelism from which will eventuate living, expanding Christian movements. The existing dictum throughout Mid-
India is that as the Mission lifts the Christian community,
it will render its most effective service toward the establishment of Christianity in the land. If there is any mission
or any mission station where this theory has been given
a thorough, devoted, intelligent trial, that mission is
the American Mennonite, and that station is Dhamtari.
As we have carefully examined this situation in the light of
the available facts, we are led to express an opinion that
in the case of these artificial, central station, Christian
communities, the above dictum must be coupled with
another. If economic improvement, intellectual development, social advance, and religious growth separate the
recipients of mission benefactions from their fellows and
make them a people apart, then for a Mission to spend
itself in the uplift of the Christian community is to defeat
its own end, creating instead a dependent, exclusive group
of individualistic Christians, frankly not interested in the
addition of others to the ranks of those for whom the
Mission is caring. If genuine progress is to be made,
steps must be taken to achieve the continual and sub-
stantial multiplication of churches. Until such growth
occurs, resources of money and personnel should be
diverted from the services of the Christians to the active

evangelization of these great castes which are so obviously open before us.

We are convinced of the impracticability of the expansion of Christianity through the careful tending of static Christian communities of non-typical people. We are troubled at the vast expenditure of love and sacrifice in a type of activity which has not led and probably will not lead to the establishment of vigorous growing Churches. The kind of Christianization carried on in Dhamtari has elsewhere in India been carried on for 100 years without significantly increasing either the size or the influence of the Christian community. We are appalled at the possibility that such should be the outcome here. We are deeply impressed with the need here for the active evangelization of the people who have elsewhere in India come to the Christian faith in groups of families, and in numbers running up into the hundreds of thousands.

We further recommend that every effort be made to help the Christian community to overcome its handicap of isolation and aloofness. The whole people movement point of view needs to be passed on to the rank and file of the Churches of Christ. The conviction that growth is essential to their existence needs to be sharpened. The willingness to identify themselves with the downtrodden and the oppressed is brought about only by an act of God's sovereign grace, for which earnest prayer ought to be offered. The active participation in evangelism amongst approachable castes by large numbers of the rank and file of the Church will only come when large numbers of the missionary and ministerial corps, men and women in evangelistic, educational, medical and philanthropic work, go regularly and enthusiastically into the

difficult work of bringing multitudes to Christ. A much-
needed activity is the training of missionaries and all
Christians in methods of personal work on a caste-wise basis
amongst the approachable peoples.

In this connection, we must call attention to the fact
that paying men and women to preach often discourages
honorary lay witnessing. It leads even missionaries to
assume that fervent "personal work" is the task of the
professional evangelist. The poison of this heresy spreads
readily. Indian colleagues, working in hospitals or other
institutions, are likely to assume that theirs is not the
task of bringing men and women to Jesus Christ—that
others with special training are paid to preach. Thus the
universal witness of every believer is eliminated and the
paid witness of a limited number of people in the evangelistic department is substituted. We venture to suggest
that an investigation as to the number of Christians who
pray daily for the conversion of certain persons and who
give some time each week to personal work with those
prayed for, would be illuminating. The way out is not
to dispense with paid evangelists and whole-time evangelistic missionaries. *The way out is for every earnest Christian,
Indian or foreign, educated or illiterate, rich or poor, to engage in
evangelistic work, preferably amongst the approachable castes as
a normal and necessary part of his Christian life. Voluntary
unpaid proclamation of the evangel by large numbers will aid in
helping the Christian community to overcome its handicap of isolation and will mean that as groups come in, they will normally
start to witness.*

We are deeply impressed by the potential resources
of Christian experience available within this Church and
Mission for such an effort as we envisage, and by the

value of such an effort for the spiritual development of
the existing Church. Indeed, the bearing of the study of
this field from the point of view of people movements
upon the wider mission field is great. The Dhamtari
study was undertaken precisely because here was a great
mission with ample resources in men and money, carefully
planning its work, and yet not sharing in the victories of
the Cross in as large a measure as were the people movement Churches. Dhamtari is more typical of the larger
mission stations of Mid-India than any other station
included in our study, and the lessons from it should be
applicable in all non-reproductive stations.

To put the matter in a nutshell, the Dhamtari Mission
is serving the Christian and non-Christian community
in the hope that somehow, some time in the future, many
will come to Christ. We believe that such is not the way
many come to Christ. We believe that many can now
come to Christ. They are found in approachable peoples,
not in the generality of the non-Christian population. When
groups of them are converted they ought to be so treated
as to make it possible for them to win some relatives, and
they in turn to spread the Gospel amongst all their relatives.

This will require the prayerful attention of the entire
Church. It calls for a major shift in emphasis without
which the same results may be expected in the future as
have occurred in the past. If this group, missionaries and
Indians alike, would turn with prayer and careful planning
to the winning of souls from approachable castes as their
major task, group movements to Christ of great significance would, we believe, result. That is the message of this
study for a devout intelligent Church where there has
never been even the beginning of a people movement.

VII

THE MEHRA PEOPLE MOVEMENT

D. A. McGavran

IN Bastar State great sal forests occupy the high ground and the fertile low lands are occupied by villages. The western and southern parts of the State are mountainous and densely forested. The eastern part, in which the Mehras live, is an upland plateau which continues without a break or any natural barrier eastward into Jaipur State.

The total population is just over 500,000. Of this 64% are Gonds of the Maria and Muria tribes. The other 36% is made up of a variety of castes. The Marias inhabit the hills in the west and south and thin out toward the eastern edge. The Mehras are an untouchable caste whose center of density lies in Jaipur State. They are fairly numerous in the eastern part of Bastar and thin out toward the west.

The Rev. C. B. Ward, an independent missionary, started the Bastar State work in 1893. Growth began soon. Figures earlier than 1905 are not available but after that the following figures give an idea of the growth of the Christian community:

1905	..	728
1910	..	1189
1918	..	1826
1923	..	2710

1927   .. 2848
1931   .. 2920
1934   .. 3882

Of this community of 3882 about 800 is now and probably has for years been living at the central station, Jagdalpur, where there is a Christian community of 100 houses or more, a hospital, a middle school, two boardings, each with about 40 students, and two bungalows. There is a fine big church. The remainder of the Christian population lives in 250 villages.

This Church arose out of a people movement among the Mehras in Jaipur State, nurtured by the Schleswig Holstein Evangelical Lutheran Mission, whose headquarters are in Kotapad. As the movement grew among the Mehras there, it spilled over into the Mehras of Bastar. Much evidence supports this view. At Kasturi on the eastern borders of Bastar State an elderly Christian said, "A Kotapad *guru* taught five of us. We went to Kotapad to be baptized. Goliyar Sahib told us that since we were of Bastar State he would not baptize us. He gave us a letter to Ward Sahib (Papa Sahib) who then baptized us." Timothy at Kasturi was asked "When you were thinking of becoming Christians did you fear that you would not be able to obtain wives for your sons and husbands for your daughters?" He answered "No Sahib, because we knew that thousands were becoming Christians over Kotapad way." Cornelius of Nagpur said, "I grew up in Silpari near Kotapad. Many of my relatives had become Christian. Then I came here and married. When the gods got after my first son and ate him up, and then when they got after my second son and he nearly died, my wife and I decided that we had better adopt this religion in which the gods and the spirits have no power." The forms of prayer and the Ooriya songs are a direct carry over from the Lutherans. The custom of calling the evangelist a guru is also Lutheran. It is significant that the number of villages in which there are Christians is greatest all along the eastern edge of Bastar where it joins Jaipur State. The number of Christians thins out toward the west and north; and though it is said that there are many Mehras in the Kondagaon Tahsil, there are few Christians there. All of which points to the Lutheran people movement as being both the source of the Bastar State movement and its continuing inspiration.

At the same time, the Bastar State Mission has not been acutely aware of the Mehra people movement. All the reports speak of the "aborigines becoming Christian," whereas the aborigines (Marias, Murias and other such tribes) have not become Christian. It is chiefly among the immigrant Mehras that Christianity has spread. A report dated 1910, states "We are working amongst the inhabitants (high castes) and the aborigines (wild tribes)." In none of the reports is there any recognition of the successful Lutheran people movement to the immediate east as having any connection with or meaning for the Bastar State work. We hazard a guess that, through the years, preaching has been carried on in all parts of the villages indiscriminately, as much to those who never became Christian as to those who were becoming Christian. There was evidently more interest in the Marias and Murias than in the Mehras, though from the Marias in forty-three years there has been only one convert, and he reverted. There has been an opinion held by the missionary group— and possibly by the Indians—that in Bastar State caste distinctions were not important. Actually caste lines are rigidly drawn. The Mehras are looked down upon by the better castes—the Bhatras, Marias, and Murias. A Bhatra Malguzar said to us, "These Mehras are a low-down lot, thieves, rascals, dirty, lying, and adulterous." Despite the failure to recognize the nature of the movement, Christianity has spread almost exclusively amongst Mehras.

An interesting and important side issue is that about 20 families each from the Ghassias, Mungias, and Mirgans, have been converted and are now living in the villages. One of the supervising ministers is from the Ghassias. Thus the people movement has in its inception established the fact that Christianity is an intercaste movement. In Jaipur about 800 Bhatras have become Christians. This Bhatra movement however stopped years ago, allegedly because the rest of the Bhatras refused to identify themselves with what was predominantly a Mehra movement.

Because the nature of the people movement was not recognized, the coming of people in groups was not stressed, and the Christian program has been weak; one finds the phenomenon of one and two Christian Mehra families in the midst of many non-Christian Mehra families. There are Christians in 250 villages. In one circuit of 23 villages, Nangur, we asked the circuit leader to name his villages and to tell how many families in each were Christian and how many non-Christian. His hasty calculation indicated that there were approximately 55 Christian families and 113 non-Christian Mehra families. Case studies revealed many Christians with non-Christian parents, brothers, sisters, brothers-in-law, sisters-in-law, uncles, and aunts. Most Christians have non-Christian cousins

and second cousins. The workers estimated that for the
area as a whole about 30 per cent of the Mehra population
has become Christian. They also judged that 30 per cent
of the Ghassias, 50 per cent of the Mungias and ten per
cent of the Mirgans have become Christian. These people
movements would appear to have plenty of scope for
growth.

The central station Christian settlement has played
an important part in the Christian movement. Lying at
the doors of the missionaries' homes, it has demanded
and received a large share of attention. Its problems have
broken the hearts of the missionaries. Its children have
in large part furnished the pupils at the central station
school. Into it have been gathered dismissed workers,
people who fled from persecution, or felt it more conven-
ient to be in the mission station, and the graduates of the
school who got jobs in Jagdalpur. It does not seem to
have much connection with the villages—though it does
have more than most central station settlements.

The central boarding schools (boys and girls) have
served to educate the children of the Christian settlement
and the workers, and to a very limited extent, village
Christians. Practically no boarding school graduate has
returned to his village. Only a few of the fifteen or so
workers are products of the boarding schools. The missionary in charge feels that for years the boarding school has
been a means of escape from the villages of Bastar State.
It would be hard to prove that the boarding school has
strengthened the Christian movement in the 250 villages.
Miss Fehr is however awake to the situation. She has
some profitable ideas in mind, amongst them that of using
the boardings to provide the housing accommodation for

adults in for short courses. The central station children also are being refused admission to the boarding though the attendance at school is encouraged. This is a healthy sign.

The language problem is central. There are several current languages. Ooriya is spoken on the eastern border. Halbi a mixture of Ooriya and Chhattisgarhi, is spoken by most people and some mission workers. The central church pastor speaks Hindi. The hymns are partly Hindi and partly Ooriya. The missionaries use only Hindi. The schools use only Hindi. The Scripture is read sometimes in Hindi and sometimes in Ooriya. The village women understand Halbi only, getting a merest glimmering from Hindi. The men get more, but if conviction is to be carried and meaning is to be made plain, the language of the people must be used.

There are now six circuits as follows:

Name of Circuit	Incharge	No. of villages	No. of Christians
Kasturi	Padre Bhan Singh	70	828
Nangur	Padre Chaitan P. John	23	212
Kirpaund	Padre Phul Chand	80	1700
Jagdalpur		18 (1 Jagdalpur)	200 800
Keslur		22	128
Kondagaon		23	162

Each of the supervising ministers has several teachers or gurus working with him. Some circuits have one, some circuits have four or five.

The worship of the groups, with the exception of three

or four centers such as Kasturi and Nangur, is rather
primitive. The Creed, Lord's Prayer, and Commandments
have been taught as baptismal requirements, but, not
having been used often in worship, have in most cases
been utterly forgotten. Even in the centers where there
are resident workers only a small fraction of the people
know these elements well enough to say them with confidence. The idea of building churches is new. Most
worship services are held in village lanes, or the court-
yard of some house, or wherever the preacher happens
to be. In the better churches the hymns are lined out, —
as are the creed and commandments. There seems to
be no set order of worship which all alike follow. Padre
Bhan Singh and Padre Phul Chand have led out in getting
people to build their own little churches. At Nangur too
is a village-built church. Padre Bhan Singh is advocating
that in each village where there are Christians there should
be a place of worship, and he points out the common custom in each village of building a "dev guri" where the
villagers assemble to worship at festival times. These dev
guris are thatched roofs on poles.

Giving is fairly general, but on a very meagre scale.
The aim of two or three annas a year per family, whether
the family be rich or poor, is set in one circuit. The workers are convinced that the people are very very poor and
cannot give much. Since most of the Christians own land,
keep pigs, and chickens, and do a bit of weaving and since
they have access to jungles for gathering mahawa blossoms,
roots and fruits and for grazing their cattle, the average
income per family is quite good as compared with other
areas. The value in rupees may be low, but the value in
kind is above average.

In order to care for the church growth which seems so likely to occur here in the future the following six steps are recommended:

1. *Understanding Group Conversion and Forwarding People Movements:*
Every English-speaking person should study Dr. Pickett's illuminating books on how churches grow by the processes of group conversion. Their bearing on this situation is very great. The message and central teachings of these books can also be presented in Hindi and the dialects to Christian students, workers and lay leaders in conferences and courses.

The people movement in Jaipur should be made the subject of careful study. Visits to the Lutheran Mehra churches should be repeatedly made. Christian leaders from the Kotapad churches should be invited to tour these Bastar State churches. In these ways knowledge of that successful growing Church, of which this is an offshoot, can be profitably spread.

Stories of how villages as a whole became Christian, and of how castes and tribes have in chains of families turned to Christ, should be written, printed and circulated widely. They might well be made part of the courses in Christian education in the church schools.

The expectation that all Mehras, Ghassias, Mirgans and Mungias will shortly become Christians should be encouraged in every way. The steady continuing growth of people movement churches in India can be a source of great cheer to these underprivileged folk.

Lists of yet unsaved relatives might well be made, and small groups in 100 villages pledged to pray for these by name each day.

2. *Establishing Christian Worship:*

Daily worship according to a simple liturgy has been found to be useful in developing a Christian consciousness among illiterate Christians. It should be possible to establish daily worship in every village where there are several families of Christians. Nothing would be better for the growth and welfare of these scattered little congregations.

The illiteracy of the villager has a vital bearing on the development of worship. The illiterate should both understand and participate in the service. It must be his service. This means, first, that the language of worship should be the language of the home. If this is Halbi then worship should be in Halbi. The worship of God should not be prostituted to the spread of Hindi. Town churches may well worship in Hindi, but Halbi-speaking congregations should be trained to worship in Halbi.

It also means that most of the materials of worship must be familiar and, indeed, practically memorized by the congregation. This in turn means a limited number of hymns, and a frequent use of memorized elements of worship like the Lord's Prayer, the Ten Commands, the Apostles Creed and passages like Romans 12:9-21.

Thirdly, it means that the use of a simple order of worship which would come to be widely known and loved would be desirable. It should be the frame on which daily and Sunday worship is organized.

Finally participation in worship will be increased if leaders adopt practices like lining out hymns, prayers, and scripture passages to be repeated phrase by phrase by the congregation. But whether by these means or others, the illiterate Christians who form such a large proportion of any people movement Church, should themselves be worshippers, intelligently participating in every aspect of their services.

3. *Training Church Leaders:*

If ingathering is to be successful, there is continuing need to train many strong, local, unpaid leaders. Each should know the worship service by heart, be committed to building a church, believe in and practice stewardship, and have a vivid idea of a great Mehra Church leading all Bastar State to the feet of Christ. These four major ideas if instilled into strong village leaders should undergird great ingathering in the coming years. It would be hoped that these leaders would take over a large share of the work of instructing the new converts, and leading them in daily worship. This would be natural for this Church. It already has an indigenous system of leadership, accepted and improved by the missionaries. We suggest simply an increased use of this fine asset.

A short course for voluntary workers is needed. A two weeks' course would be feasible but if this could be stretched out to one month it would be even better. If possible a women's section too ought to be held. In a month's course it should be possible to teach many to read by the Laubach method.

The Church however needs more than part time voluntary workers. It needs paid workers who are literate, who will be supported by the people and who come of the people themselves. To this end young men should be sought out and brought in to Jagdalpur for six months' training. They should understand clearly that they go back to a village center, preferably one which has agreed already to contribute generously to the support of a pastor-teacher; and that their living will depend largely upon the villagers themselves. The Mission might at first give a small grant to supplement what a group of fifty families perhaps does not yet give. The training and successful location of twenty such workers in the next two years, and the training of much larger numbers in the future we consider desirable.

In certain places teachers are already at work in non-Christian Maria villages drawing their entire support from the people. Every effort should be expended toward getting Christian teachers similarly located in Christian groups.

4. *Self-Support:*

As ingathering takes place, it should be on the basis of self-support. As people become inquirers, the Church should let them know that Christians give largely. New villages especially can be led to give largely. To some extent this means the conversion of the existing Christian community to self-support. But in larger measure it means that new conditions are laid down for those who become Christians from now on. All preaching should include vivid descriptions of self-support, people proud of self-support, people refusing to be beggars, people building their own churches, the Mehra people on fire with a sense of mission, and called of God to build the New Jerusalem on the highlands of Bastar State.

God's ghara, God's acre, a tenth of the chickens, and pigs, and rice, and earnings are all good methods of achieving self-support.

Even more desirable, however, is getting some workers whose income is dependent on the gifts of the people. As long as the people know that the Mission will not let "its" worker suffer, they will not give. Why should they?

The basic fact that the Christians of Bastar State are comparatively well off needs to replace the existing thought that the Bastar people are the poorest in India. Measured in kind their condition is probably superior to that of Christians of many parts of India.

5. *Concentration on Village:*

The future of the Christian Movement in Bastar State is in the villages. It is not in the central station. The center of attention then should be the villages. The central station ought to get no more attention, time, prayer and worry than any other four or five hundred of the Christian community receive. Indeed, it should get less, since it has in its literate membership a far greater potential leadership. It could be committed into the hands of some capable leader who will have complete control and responsibility, with consultation concerning local problems no more often than Padre Bhan Singh or Padre Phul Chand at Kasturi and Kirpaund have. The emancipation of the church forces from the central station settlement is very desirable. It will not come naturally. It must be consciously sought.

6. *The Marias and Murias:*

The immediate task is the extension of the Kingdom amongst the Mehras, the building of a strong, self-supporting, constantly worshipping Church from amongst them. Toward this end 95 per cent of the time and attention of the Christian forces should go. The hope of the extension of the Kingdom lies principally in the establishment of that Church. The surest way to win the Marias and Murias is to build a victorious Mehra church.

This Church with fifteen workers, two fine boarding schools, a new insight into how great populations are Christianized and a successful growing Church as its next door neighbor, faces a brilliant future. God will use these Christian forces to bring in thousands. The call of these days is to understand people movements and to extend the Church among the approachable peoples of this fertile highland, confident that it will bring them abundant and eternal life.

VIII

POSSIBLE SATNAMI PEOPLE MOVEMENTS

J. W. Pickett

IN Raipur we came to the headquarters of the work of the Evangelical Synod of North America. From Raipur we went to Bishrampur, the first Evangelical Mission station in Chhattisgarh, and one which has exercised a profound influence on the Satnamis' understanding of the Christian program. Baitalpur, another station, the center of the chief group of village Christians from amongst the Satnamis within the sphere of this mission, was also visited. There is at present no revival amongst the Satnamis, and no group movements at all have occurred amongst them in this territory for the last twenty years. However they are the principal "untouchable" caste in Chhattisgarh. The problem here therefore is to determine why movements in these areas have been arrested and how this ripened field can be harvested.

A brief statement about the Satnamis will be necessary to understand the situation. These people number 500,000 of whom by far the larger part, probably 450,000 live in Chhattisgarh. The Satnamis were originally Rohidas Chamars. A certain Ghasi Das in 1830 started a religious movement amongst them, which soon attained great proportions. Since that time there has been a constant stream of groups leaving the idolatrous Rohidas Chamar religion for the religion of Satnam, the True Name. The

movement was partly a revolt against caste oppression
and the domination of the Brahmans, and partly an attempt
to struggle up the social ladder by giving up liquor, tobacco, meat, and idolatry. The one "True Name," "Satnam,"
was both the only object of worship and the ordinary
greeting. There is a tradition that Ghasi Das got his
basic idea of giving up idoltary and worshipping the True
Name from Christian missionaries in Cuttack when he was
on pilgrimage to the temple of Jagganath at Puri. He
foretold the coming of a white man with a large umbrella-
like hat, with the Book of the True Name under his arm,
and instructed his followers to believe the new teaching
when it came.

The Satnamis are peasants. Quite a large number
own from two to four acres of land. Probably 10% of
them own 10 or more acres of land. A few are feudal
lords, (malguzars) but the number of these is decreasing.
A large per cent are landless labourers. The Satnamis are
regarded as untouchables, and live in separate sections of
the villages or in separate villages. Satnamism has not
redeemed them from the Chamar name or from the many
typical oppressed classes' sins and weaknesses. They are
for the most part illiterate and indifferent to learning.
Ghasi Das' revolt against Hinduism did not go far enough.
Idol worship has crept back in. Were not Christianity
the logical outcome of the Satnami reform, the community
would likely become just another "Untouchable" Hindu
caste; though with the new passion of Hinduism to retain
"Untouchable" votes there is a strong movement to lift
the community to the level of a low Sudra caste. The
leadership of the Satnamis places its hope in education
and the achieving of Sudra status. Perhaps therefore the

best aspect of contemporary Church history to present to the Satnami for the purpose of inclining them to Christ would be the movement among Sudras in Andhra Pradesh to enter the Church of Christ.

The history of the growth of the Christian movement among members of this promising and enterprising caste is replete with lessons. Work first started when the Rev. O. Lohr came to Chhattisgarh, bought 1600 acres of land at Bishrampur in 1868 and began to tour and preach. He received an enthusiastic welcome from the leaders of the Satnamis, and it looked at first as if the whole caste would become Christian. When, however, they discovered that a change of life was expected, and that polygamy and lustful practices were forbidden, the Satnami leaders became definitely indifferent, if not hostile. From then on individual converts were won with a fair degree of regularity over a very wide territory—Mr. Lohr and his associates toured extensively. These came almost always from amongst the Satnamis. We closely questioned 16 of the oldest residents of Bishrampur and Baitalpur. The conversion pattern in each case was the same. The story of Timothy Loknath as translated by the Rev. M. P. Davis is typical. "My uncle Phirto *went to Bishrampur* to visit his brother Paulus Munshi, (who *had gone there* previously) saw how the Christians lived there, came back, turned over his land to my father and *went to Bishrampur* with his family. Not long after my brother Lute came to get us also. We desired to sell our land to the landlord, who said, 'Don't go. Remain here.' But at last we sold to him. There were nine of us, four brothers, three sisters, and parents. Taking two small children on his shoulders father *went* with us and our things *to Bishrampur* May 5, 1880." (*The italics are ours.*)

This deliberate policy was dictated by a belief that it was impossible for the Satnami to remain in his village and lead the Christian life. Isolated Christians remained ignorant of Christian truth, were practically never able to participate in Christian worship, and under the pressure of caste and heathendom either lapsed morally or apostacised. Therefore converts were encouraged to come in, were given land and work, so that while earning their own living, they could be instructed in the faith, educated, disciplined, and made into good Christians. While it is true that this policy built up a devout, church-going and intelligent Christian community of hundreds at Bishrampur, it also established clearly in the minds of lay-Christians and non-Christians, that becoming a Christian meant—(a) leaving one's people and going to live at the mission settlement; (b) leaving one's feudal lord and becoming the follower of the benevolent Padre Sahib, who thereupon became at least partly responsible to see that his followers had work and enough to eat; (c) living a life free from persecution in a community richly served by foreign funds (schools, dispensary, famine relief, etc.); (d) accepting the Christian religion in place of the Satnami faith.

On top of this fatal land colony experience came the famine in 1897-1900. The conviction that Christianity, as seen at Bishrampur, was a good thing, had been growing steadily, especially in villages near Bishrampur and Baitalpur; and when the special stimulus of hard times came, large numbers were baptised. Dr. J. Gass said to us of this famine period, "Many, possibly as many as 2000, were baptised. Practically all were Satnamis. Probably 600 went back, and 1000 moved to Baitalpur and Bishrampur. Many went to Calcutta and elsewhere."

Sixty-three families from eight villages from within 5 miles of Bishrampur were baptised and remained Christians for several years. These expected no doubt the same benefits which the Bishrampur community received. They did receive work and help during the famine. When, after the famine, relief work ceased, when the movement grew so big that all could not receive the personal paternal care of the missionary, when Lohr Sahib, whose benevolent rule through famine times had endeared him to many, suddenly died, and when the Hindu landlords seeing that Lohr Sahib was dead began again to threaten, oppress and persecute the village Christians, then the village Christians living outside of Bishrampur apostacised. Today Bishrampur stands alone with no group of Christians living in the villages in which they were converted.

The villages around Baitalpur fared better, possibly because there was less land to give out, and possibly because there was no abrupt change of regime at a critical time. There remain today four villages with two to eight Christian peasant families in each. But none of these groups grew after 1904. Near Raipur was a small movement at Jora, which persists to this day, but which, in the 38 years without accessions from the outside, has become "a group apart" with little vital connection with the Satnami community.

A third factor in determining the mind-set of the present-day Satnami was the orphanage-reared Christian boy and girl. Together with the famine, there came into the mission a large number of famine orphans. These and the children of the Christians were served with utmost love and devotion. This mission has always stressed education. The best training available, at that time up to the 7th

Hindi, was provided for the orphans. Funds, personnel
and other resources of the mission were absorbed by the
orphanages. Many children were cared for by the mission
for eight, some for twelve, and some for even eighteen and
twenty years. The resulting Christians were completely
divorced from their own people, their villages, their customs.
They were peculiarly dependent on the mission. The result
was a loosely integrated community bound together chiefly
by their common relation as beneficiaries of the mission.
Those not in mission service frequently felt aggrieved, and
were called "outsiders" by those in mission service. There
was a good deal of friction in Bishrampur and Baitalpur,
especially when paternalism came to be recognized as an
evil and people were encouraged to stand on their own feet.
As for the Hindus and Satnamis on the outside, these
orphanage and boarding school products failed to impress
them, except as a people consenting to profess the Christian
religion in return for rich services received.

In their turn it was difficult for the Christians to
imagine any one becoming a full-fledged Christian unless
he, too, came to live in the artificially enriched soil of the
Christian settlement. Spontaneous evangelism of Satnamis by their Christian relatives grew less and less.

An element in the situation, of which account must
be taken, is the system of village primary schools which
has been established. There are 45 schools with a total
enrollment of about 4400. Of these about 800 are Depressed Classes children and 3600 are the children of Caste
Hindus. Some missionaries think of this effort as purely
social service, disinterestedly helping forward the cause of
education in this backward section. "Illiteracy is a greater
evil than leprosy. From the evangelistic standpoint, fight-

ing these evils may not seem important, but from the
Christian standpoint, in the service of the people, we must
address ourselves to this problem, if no one else is doing
it," wrote one. The majority of the missionaries to whom
we talked, however regarded schools as a form of evangelistic effort. Bible is regularly taught and one missionary
expressed the opinion that, though neither had won many
converts, the schools were a better evangelizing agency
than the evangelists, in that the work was more regular,
was better supervised, was carried on by better trained
men and with more impressionable material. Assuming
that the ultimate justification of these schools depends
upon whether they help to build a great vital Church, we
are compelled to call attention to the fact that primary
schools for non-Christians have not won large groups of
men to Christ. Rather the evidence is that, in circumstances such as these, mission village schools for non-
Christians have actually hardened their pupils, so that
when revival has spread through the territory, it has left
Christians everywhere except in those villages occupied by
a mission school. In these days when ingathering of adults
by the hundreds is taking place all over India and
in particular in four stations within 70 to 200 miles of
Raipur, the school process, which requires that those
influenced grow to manhood before they decide for Christ,
is far too gradual. To conclude: if the schools are to be
justified as social service projects, that is one thing; but
we are convinced that they have not and will not initiate
great ingathering of the approachable castes. Pinning
hope for the growth of the Church in the villages to numerous government grant-in-aid schools is, we consider,
to a considerable extent responsible for the present static

situation. The enrollment in these schools is 82 per cent Hindu and where Hindus predominate in the classes the atmosphere is rarely favorable to Christian evangelism.

The experiences recounted in the previous paragraphs have been most discouraging to the Christian staff at work in these stations. Long, devoted and intelligent labors have been rewarded by considerable reversions. The Christian community which does remain is aggrieved at a mission which no longer considers its primary duty the material support of the Christian community. Eudcational and evangelistic efforts have been less fruitful than was expected. Thus there is a tendency to produce in some of the Christian leaders a belief that the Satnami Chamar is of too poor stuff to make a vital Christian Church. To the extent that such a belief is seriously entertained, it very greatly prejudices the chance for a revivifying Christian movement among the Satnamis. Consequently we desire to point out that many castes more ignorant and uncivilized, more sinful and degraded, more stunted by oppression and untouchability have in people movements been redeemed by the grace of God, and have developed into strong indigenous Christian Churches. It is also true that the history of the self improvement of these people who completely gave up idols, tobacco, the keeping of pigs, chickens and goats, the eating of certain vegetables, and to a large extent the eating of meat of any sort, who achieved a considerable degree of organization, and have maintained it in the face of foes without and within, is indicative of great potential ability. While, therefore, we can readily understand how a belief in the utter inferiority of the Satnamis should have arisen, we are convinced that serious thought will, on the contrary,

convince most people that the Satnami is well above
the average amongst the oppressed class people of India
today.

This analysis of the situation as seen from the point
of view of possible caste-wise ingathering has been stated
at some length because the situation is one more or less
common to all Mission stations in Chhattisgarh, but chiefly because the possibilities for caste-wise revival amongst
the Satnamis must be viewed against the background of
the existing situation. With that as analysed, what should
be done to co-operate with the Spirit of God, who elsewhere in India is bringing 125,000 to 200,000 of the
oppressed classes a year into the abundant life in Christ
Jesus? What should be done to help make abundant life
through the Church the possession of these oppressed
shepherdless "True Name" Chamars? At the outset we
would state that since people movements are brought about
by the Holy Spirit, it must not be imagined that they can
be induced by close thinking, good organization and hard
work alone. Nevertheless the Mass Movement Study has
revealed certain facts concerning the way in which God has
redeemed numerous peoples and has built great Churches.
From amongst these facts, those which seem especially
important in relation to this situation are herewith presented in the belief that following them consistently for a
period of years will greatly increase the chances of vigorous
Church growth.

First comes that unquestioned fact, that certain peoples
are prepared by God for a widespread response at a given
time to His Word. The "Untouchables" and Aborigines
of India give every indication of being such peoples and
this is the time for their response. The Satnamis are the

most numerous of the "Untouchables" of Chhattisgarh and, to date, the caste from which there has been the greatest number of converts. We believe that they are a people prepared by God to accept His Son in this generation.

Another most important fact in the growth of the Church has been an indomitable faith that God wills the salvation of those who are responding to His Call. We believe that an essential factor in renewed ingathering from amongst the Satnamis is a heightened faith that God's grace can and will operate amongst this approachable people, so uniquely prepared for the Gospel, who are so nearly ready to accept Him, and from whom have already come 5000 or more Christian men and women. God's arm is not shortened. These Satnamis are part and parcel of the oppressed hosts who throughout India are restlessly pondering the proposal of leaving bondage and starting the march to Canaan. It is true that the control of the caste through *bhandaris* and *mahants*, a control centralized in the *gurus* at Bhandar, is an obstacle. But the obstacles on the road out of Egypt have again and again been overcome by the power of God, and can be so overcome here too. God is greater than Pharaoh.

Of particular importance is what the Satnami or other approachable person unconsciously believes "becoming a Christian" to mean. It goes without saying that the central Christian message is Jesus Christ crucified for sinful men. That is the message preached by Evangelicals all through the years. That is the only message which will win men to the changed life. But under the existing circumstances, extreme care must be taken to see that this glorious message does not mean to the listener that "the individual for benefits received goes to the mission

settlement to get saved and leaves his relatives and former comrades to get along as best they can unsaved." Our
conversations with Satnamis in the vicinity of Raipur,
Bishrampur, Janjgir, Dhamtari and Mungeli convince us
that this individualistic pattern dominates their thinking.
It dominates it even in remote sections of the plain, but is
especially true within twenty miles of any mission station.
So while the center of the Christian message must and will
remain the cross, the periphery must be such that the fatal
individualistic pattern is superseded by the group pattern.
To erase the harmful marginal learnings, acquired inci-
dentally from the conduct of the Christian enterprise, and
not from any plan of the Christian leaders, will require
careful re-education of workers, Indian and non-Indian,
and of lay Christians to the group movement point of view.
This means not merely reviewing the lessons we have here
presented, but also consciously eliminating from the preaching and teaching illustrations of people who were converted, left their villages and were educated in central station
schools. All materials which even inadvertently assume or
imply that people will probably not become Christians,
that if they do they will leave their villages, that they will
find themselves out of the old social group, that they will
have to marry into the central station Christian group, or
that their children will go away to school, lead as a rule in
the wrong direction. Conversely, the Christian message
should be presented to the accompaniment of a series of
vivid pictures of great caste movements to Christ, of individuals staying in their own homes amidst much persecution and by the witness of their victorious lives leading their
families and caste fellows to Christ, of Christians forming
little churches in remote villages far from any mission aid,

of people who became followers not for education or uplift, but for salvation, of village chapels built by the people themselves, and of ordinary villagers transformed by God's grace and made great leaders in growing and victorious village churches. *The teaching of abundant current material of this sort to his workers is the duty of every superintending minister.* The continual use of such victorious illustrations by the preachers and the missionaries amongst the people of approachable castes will do much to encourage contagious reproductive Christian decisions.

A most important task will be that of helping the Hindi-speaking Christian community see and adopt the revival and ingathering point of view, and another that of firing them with the belief that in these days they can expect God to bring in their relatives and friends.

The Evangelical Mission is fortunate in having a strong revival in progress amongst the Garas to the south and east of the Satnami field. This should be of much value in demonstrating to the Satnamis the group pattern of accepting Christ, as opposed to the non-reproductive individual pattern. Strategy lies in using the Gara revival in and around Basna to light fires in the Satnami settlements lying adjacent to the region of the Gara awakening. From this point of view we feel that the Pithora field is of great importance. While we were unable to visit this, we talked to the Rev. M. M. Paul, the person in charge, and the account he brings of the group movement of Satnamis under Prem Das, a former *maha*.*t*, is encouraging. In April 1934, Prem Das, his uncle and his brother-in-law, twelve people in all, professed the Christian faith. Three months later Prem Das won five of his cousins. In March 1935 nine other relatives joined this small Christian group. Other accessions have since taken place and interest is running high amongst the Satnamis for miles around. We believe that the Pithora field will repay additional support and a close application of people movement methods. For the person in charge to visit the Baptist and Mennonite Gara Churches frequently and to study the growth of the Church there would be distinctly helpful.

In close connection with this is the desirability of carrying the Gara revival north and east from Basna. There are considerable numbers of Garas living scattered through this territory and nothing will hasten a revival amongst the Satnamis more than the example of their Gara neighbors becoming Christians on group lines.

Finally we recommend that there be widespread and continued prayer for ingathering; that amongst all, Indian and non-Indian, prayer bands be formed of those who will covenant to pray for revival amongst the Satnamis and other approachable castes such as the Garas and Mahars, that supporters in other lands be asked for prayer; that individuals and villages and beginning group movement be made the object of widespread prayer. In a day of great opportunity amongst one of the most accessible people in India we believe that the group approach will encourage decisions for Christ which will multiply and reproduce themselves; but we are convinced that the spiritual power needed to initiate any such vast movement will be supplied only as people pour themselves out in directed prayer for the salvation of these five hundred thousand Satnamis who are so near to the Kingdom.

IX

WHEN THE CHURCH GROWS

D. A. McGavran

WHEN the Church grows greatly how does it grow? How does such growth start? Can a Central Station Tradition start growing churches? Once a growing Church is established, how is it best nurtured? These four questions probe deeply into the whole subject of church growth. They will be considered one by one.

But before we can tackle them satisfactorily we shall have to deal with an objection. "In all this consideration of church growth," it will be said, "are we not forgetting that growth, and perhaps the most important growth, has nothing to do with numerical increase at all?"

We need to define what we mean by growth. There is growth in grace and growth in wisdom. Both are being achieved in all 145 stations of Mid-India. When we speak here of "church growth," however, we do not mean the spiritual or intellectual advance of existing members of static central station churches. Our study is concerned with the expansion of Christianity. It was precisely the deep dissatisfaction of the Christian leadership of Mid-India with 12% per decade increase in membership, accompanied though this was by a considerable degree of advance in wisdom and grace which led the Provincial Christian Council to inaugurate this study. The idea that in the midst of spiritually hungry multitudes, there can be "spiritual" growth permanently divorced from conversion

increase, seems deficient to us. Much thinking about
spiritual growth on the mission field assumes that "given
spiritual growth numerical increase will automatically
follow."¡ Evidence does not support this assumption.
The careful tending of congregations of non-typical persons, their great increase in wisdom and grace, in health
and productivity, in maturity and evangelistic encounter
with their environment has not anywhere in Mid-India
produced significant numerical increase. None of the
growing churches we have described has been born through
a central station community being perfected to the place
where it started spontaneously to expand.

By "church growth" we mean a process of spiritual
reproduction whereby new congregations are formed.
The Church in New Testament times grew in this fashion.
New congregations by the score sprang up where there had
been none before. In our use of the term, a Church "grows"
when it multiplies its membership and its congregations
and then with ever-increasing power takes into itself
converts in a widening stream.

With this understood, we ask our first question. How
does the Church grow when it grows greatly?

It grows within some social stratum. If to the necessary difficulties of denying self and following the Lord Jesus
are added the unnecessary abandoning of one's own race
(caste in Mid-India) and joining another, then church
growth will inevitably be slow. Great growth has almost
always been caste-wise. When the Church has made its
greatest strides, individuals became Christian with their
fellow tribesmen, with their kindred and with their people.
This is the pentecostal pattern. We hesitate to think what
might have happened, if on Pentecost, Peter had required

as a first step in following Christ, a willingness to dine with pig-eating Gentiles. But he did no such thing. Jews could become Christian with no consciousness of traitorously abandoning their people. Consequently for many years the number of disciples increased—indeed the Bible says it multiplied. On the strength of this, we might say that when the number of the disciples multiples, it usually does so within some one people.

Not only so, but multiplication usually occurs within some prepared people. One of our basic assumptions is that God prepares certain peoples to accept His Son. The Biblical illustrations of this truth are numerous. It is impossible to imagine the growth of the Christian religion without Israel, the Chosen, the Prepared People. Then too, the condition of the Roman empire, the state of civilization 1900 years ago, and the unique contribution of the Greeks conspire to make us believe that God prepares peoples to believe on the Lord Jesus Christ. He has been preparing peoples in India. It appears reasonable that ingathering will occur among those castes in Mid-India which have elsewhere in India turned to Jesus Christ.

If our evangelism is to bear the richest fruit these two basic assumptions should be considered in their varied aspects. If the Gospel is preached to such peoples, chains of families may be expected to decide for Christ. Churches will be built up in which social solidarity has not been impaired. That God has prepared a given people practically never means that the entire people, of say forty thousand souls, becomes Christian on a certain day. It does mean, however, that the atmosphere in the caste is such that today a group of five families is baptized after suitable instruction and that in succeeding months other families of this caste, who are relatives of these first, are also baptized in groups. Thus the movement gradually grows from among the people prepared by God for exodus from the land of bondage. In the course of some years the "forty thousand" may be baptized.

Our second question is: How does growth within a people begin? How do group conversions start? Let us first consider the situation when the Christian message has a fresh field in which to work. As the Gospel is preached by new-comers or foreigners, as it always must be in the beginning, it is received with curiosity, courtesy, anger, or ridicule as the case may be, but always with a very partial understanding of what it means. If the preacher is a foreign missionary, fighting against the handicap of an imperfect knowledge of the language, customs, beliefs, and traditions of a complex civilization, then the lack of understanding is magnified. Some time, possibly some years, may pass before anyone will place sufficient faith on this reputed Savior to entrust his life to Him. Sooner or later, however, a man or woman is converted. In a few more years perhaps fifty others have followed the first one. If a majority of these individuals are from one people, then the preacher has found the people prepared by God and group accessions to the Christian faith may well begin. Indeed, the fabric of society is such that long before fifty have accepted Jesus as Lord, the enquirers will have come in small groups.

What is done with these first converts is a matter of critical importance. Either the group tendency will be encouraged or discouraged by the preacher. Either he will impose an examination on all members of the group and admit only those who pass the examination as individuals, thus breaking up the natural units and stressing the one-by-one pattern. Or he will count the admission to Christian faith of as large and functional a social unit as possible the more important matter, and will so instruct as to preserve and enhance social solidarity.

Persecution in some form may be assumed. It will be difficult for the converts to continue in their old homes and to earn their living at old occupations. If circumstances drive them away from their people and means of livelihood, so that they become financially dependent on the mission, which proceeds to make provision for their employment; then, whatever statements to the contrary are made, men will believe that becoming Christian means being cared for by the benevolent mission. If the employment offered is that of preaching of the Gospel, the conclusion will be drawn (doubtless unjustly in most cases) that becoming a Christian is a means to a livelihood. If in addition to the converts, orphans are admitted to orphanages, and the blind, the lame and the halt are accepted in various types of benevolent homes, the impression will become indelible that becoming a Christian means adopting a new and kindlier "father and mother;" and that only the indigent, the orphans, the naked, hungry or homeless become Christian. That this impression is a false one will make no difference. It will be believed just the same.

It is possible that, where walls of opposition tower up into the sky, making this kind of convert, trying to weed out those who come for jobs and bread, but accepting those who seem sincere and making provision for them, may be the only way to proceed. We recognize that there are such places, though not in Mid-India. However, a consideration of the ultimate outcomes in the type of church created make us believe. that it is better to spend years preaching the Gospel, accepting no individual converts, working and waiting and praying for a group of people to become Christian together, endure persecution, receive no financial aid from the mission, continue in their former occupations and former homes, and look to Jesus the Author and Perfecter of their faith; rather than to permit the other conversion pattern to be established.

What happens where the other conversion pattern has already been established? How does the Church grow within the people prepared by God when a central station congregation has long existed and years of mission station labours have stamped in a pattern of conversion by extraction? This is the third question and the problem which faces Mid-India and many other mission fields.

It has sometimes happened that central station mission work has continued its quiet institutional way with its very slow growing congregation made up of occasional converts and rescued persons, until, without the staff intending it, striving for it, or even understanding it, some man was converted who because of his strong caste loyalty refused to let either "persecution by his village" or "Christianzation by extraction" separate him from his kindred. He continued to live with them, bear their reproaches, convince them that he was still of them, and explain why he had become a Christian. Sometimes he failed to persuade any to share his faith. In such cases he either died a lone Christian or reverted to caste. Sometimes he induced his family and close caste neighbours and relations to become Christian. In such cases the central station had given to it the unsought beginning of a people movement.

In most cases of unsought beginnings of group conversions the central station did not recognize them as pearls
of great price. Often no one was assigned to live with and
lead the group of new converts. They were "shepherded"
by weekly, monthly or even annual visits from the central
station miles away. Often when a worker was assigned to
them, he was a man of central station upbringing who had
little understanding of the inner workings of the caste concerned, little sympathy with the tremendous problems
faced by the new group, and no experience of village life.
Seldom were leaders from the new converts trained fast
enough. Usually, neither was enough Christian truth
taught them, nor enough worship provided, so that they
grew in grace. Whereas in the beginning stages of a central station, one missionary to ten and twenty Christians has been provided; a small part of one missionary's
time and budget has been considered sufficient for the care
of scores, hundreds or even thousands, of "village Christians." The institutional work has usually seemed more
important than the care of backward groups of villagers.
If under this system the village churches survived, well
and good. If they did not, "group conversion" had another
black mark chalked up against it!

How could such a system grow up? There are two
reasons. First, to give an untried beginning serious and
skilful care is risky. Even if given sufficient attention, it
may collapse. Even if sufficiently nourished, it may not
thrive. Its degree of inherent vigor varies. A small group
may have become Christian because of special circumstances when caste-wide preparation is incomplete. Or
the caste may have a system of ostracism which effectively
stops further growth. If the missionary leaves his central

station work, congregation, and residence to live in a distant village where a hundred souls have come to Christian faith and despite his efforts the new group reverts, the central station tradition anywhere in Mid-India would judge the missionary ill-advised, impulsive, and irresponsible.

Second, the difference in "growth potential" between the central station and people movement varieties of congregation is almost never recognized by the central station workers. The central station church, depending on Christianization by extraction has a very low growth potential. The group conversion church has a high growth potential. The one cannot multiply, the other can. Yet, the central station church, (educated, at the very doors of the workers, and tractable because so many of its members are employed in church or mission enterprises) appears to be a much better proposition than the people movement beginning (made up of illiterates, in hard-to-reach villages, fresh out of a non-Christian system, and not tractable by considerations of employment). Thus the lion's share of time, attention, prayer, budget, school and hospital opportunity is usually given to the church which cannot grow by spontaneous expansion.

The best that can be said for this system is that it provides a stern test of converted groups. It is our conviction, however, that a stern test is not required, but rather to recognize that the central station exists in order that when such a beginning occurs it be given skilled nurture and expanded. This is what the church and mission were established to do. When "churches which can grow" are born, the static central station church has found its chief task. When a company for drilling wells strikes oil, its job is to care for the flowing well, not just to go on drilling.

We have spoken above of the unsought beginnings of group conversions, which occasionally have occurred in this mission station. Are the Churches and Missions then shut up to quiet labour in the central station tradition until these unsought beginnings happen? We do not think so. We believe that the central station churches can seek group conversions, help induce group conversions, and when they occur so shepherd them that infant mortality amongst them is cut to a minimum.

The steps that we propose are no cure-all. There is no magic formula by which churches start growing. Only God can produce the people-wide readiness to leave the land of bondage which is essential to any considerable people movement church. But surely we may assume, as we see great Churches of hundreds of thousands of souls arising elsewhere in India and many beginning movements occurring in Mid-India that God is producing people-wide readiness in many castes. The steps we propose seem to us to be ways of co-operating with the Holy Spirit so that the central station churches so educated, so blessed, so Christian, may break out of their static condition and start "multiplying people movement churches" in their vicinities. We know of no other way in which these missions and churches, marked with a 12% per decade growth, can start congregations which will grow by spontaneous expansions. Should other ways be found, no one would rejoice more greatly than ourselves. But till they are found we suggest that these steps be tried.

The temptation will be not to try these steps but to go on doing "accustomed mission work." We are impelled to say that no mere continuation of traditional church and mission methods will win peoples, even prepared peoples, to Christ. We have seen again and again how the central station tradition while saving individuals has lost peoples, arrested growing movements, and focussed attention on procedures which do not multiply congregations. We believe that mission work of the traditional variety— the rich services of a static central station congregation, plus much evangelism, medicine, education and agriculture to the general public—can neither encourage the tender beginnings of caste-wise ingathering to appear nor recognize them if they did. Yet we believe that if these great Churches and Missions with ample resources in Christian experience and deep dedication reorient themselves toward caste-wise movements to Christian faith, they can play an important part in starting and shepherding mighty growing Churches and thus share in the victories of the Cross in much larger measure than now seems possible. We hope that the very enumeration of the following seven steps will illumine still further the problem of how static churches may start growing churches. That is a central problem of Missions and Churches around the world.

First it is to be remembered that Christianization by extraction has created a Christian Church, which in comparison with its origins is a miracle. This miracle is not hid from the world. Its witness is clear that Jesus saves. Here are found hundreds of earnest faithful Christians. Here is regular Christian worship. Church bells ring out across the land. Here are innumerable contacts with the people of the country. Here is not only a translated Bible, but a Bible in the hearts of Christian witnesses. Once the unsuspected handicaps under which this community labours—namely that it forms a separate people and is inclined to make becoming a Christian mean "leaving your kindred and joining our church"—has been clearly seen, it should be possible to overcome it.

Second, to this community, in which are many devout men and women actively longing for the spread of God's Kingdom, should be given the facts concerning the growth of the Church by group conversions in peoples prepared by God. The light as to how peoples become Christian should be made available in the vernacular in every non-multiplying Church where Christianization by extraction is the prevailing pattern. The people movement described in Acts should be carefully studied. Vernacular editions of this book and Pickett's books should be taught at annual institutes. Visits to successful people movement Churches should be arranged, with much opportunity to speak on their return. Teams from adjoining people movements should be brought in to tell of the victories of Christ through caste-wide revivals. The non-growing community should be led to see the group conversion pattern and recognize it as a normal and desirable way of Christianization.

Third, as the community comes to recognize that the goal is group ingathering from among some approachable people, voluntary evangelism along people lines should be stressed. Often, where the existing Christians have come largely from some approachable caste, the relatives of members furnish the most natural objective. "Relatives Day" can be observed. Special letters to relatives can be printed leaving spaces for the sender to sign his name and to write in the name of the uncle, aunt, cousin or in-law to whom he is sending the missive. Such letters, in rural areas, will have to be delivered by hand. A planned persistent campaign, year after year, amongst relatives is often the best approach. If the Christians are at a loss to know which are the people from which ingathering might be possible, it would be well to remember that castes responsive elsewhere, are likely to be responsive locally; and that those from which many individual Christians have come are likely to be those from which group conversion could begin.

Fourth, full time church and mission workers—teachers, compounders, preachers, women evangelists, pastors, elders, missionaries—can be led to concentrate on the peoples who are adjudged prepared by God. Evangelistic efforts among these should be redoubled. Personal work by physicians, teachers, laymen, and pastors among individuals from these peoples in schools, hospitals, factories, and places of business should be encouraged. This is a day to stress soul winning by every Christian. The New Testament churches spread when even those who were scattered abroad by persecution at Jerusalem went everywhere witnessing to their Lord. "Every Christian an evangelist among people who can be won and organized into congregations" is the great need. The Church needs to evangelize where the Holy Spirit has prepared for Himself a people of God.

Fifth, through all these efforts, whose consummation may take some years, there should be singleness of aim,—group ingathering in which individuals will be able to resist social dislocation and continue to earn their living in their former fashion. There should be prayer for group conversions, work for group conversions, and witness of group conversions. Christians should visualize vividly the kind of ingathering wanted and focus attention on that. That kind of congregation should be preached and pictured and prayed for. It is not an easy thing to do, for what the Christians, both national and non-national know by experience is Christianization by extraction. That is also what the people know, to whom the message is taken. What is known by first hand is therefore to be laid aside— that the mission rears indigent children, the convert leaves his village, the church gives work to new Christians, the mission educates children, becoming a Christian is taking on a new and kindlier overlord; and what is known through books or visits is to be proclaimed—that men and women in groups and by common consent become disciples, live on where they have always lived, bear patiently any persecution which may befall, worship God every evening, and support their minister liberally. To achieve the proclamation of this new pattern volunteers, pastors, and elders need careful training in witness. Too frequently the witness of central station Christians is likely to be something like this: "Why did I become a Christian? You threw me out. These kind people took me in, cared for me, healed me, gave me a valuable and expensive education for my children. If you ever get thrown out, remember the Christians." The supervising minister will need to spend much time listening to preaching and witness, and correcting it when it proclaims or assumes the wrong pattern. He needs to teach his congregation and his evangelists what to say, so that their message may be that Scriptural Word which will create sturdy, independent and growing congregations.

Some tracts either explicitly or implicitly expect the "individual becomes a Christian and separates from his people" type of conversion; so new tracts should be written and published, which picture conversion in people

movement terms. We are only beginning to see that becoming disciples of Christ does not need to denationalize
and dislocate. The full picture is yet hidden from us.
The rich heritage of India's peoples should be conserved.
Surely the most natural way to conserve it is for castes and
peoples, practicing those portions of the heritage which
are theirs, to move into Christian faith in sufficiently large
social units so that their social life continues and is indeed
enhanced. Tracts picturing this kind of conversion need
to be written.

Sixth, it seems desirable that in areas where group
conversions are possible, churches and missions hesitate
long before baptizing lone men or women, who turn up
at a mission station, are likely to become charges on the
church, will probably become paid evangelists in a short
while, or are going to be sent for training immediately.
Baptizing such individuals means practicing the wrong
pattern while proclaiming the right one. Sincere inquirers
should be helped to win their families and caste-fellows,
and then the group baptized together. Occasionally some
strong individual who has failed to win his fellows before
baptism but who believes that he can win them after
baptism, should be baptized. We are not trying to induce
individuals to renounce their people, but to get groups
who remain in vital relationship with their people to
accept Jesus Christ as Lord and Saviour.

Seventh, sometime, in connection with such a conscious
seeking or entirely unsought, a group of families will apply
for admission to the Church. This group is the pearl of
great price. If it is successfully shepherded, it should grow
with great vigor. It constitutes a new variety of church.
Correctly tended it has almost limitless possibilities of

expansion. Consequently, it should be given the very best spiritual care, especially in the weeks and months following baptism. Material care should be most sparingly given. The caste fellows of these new Christians, especially those connected by blood and marriage will be the most responsive people in the entire district. They would be made the special object of prayer and witness. The results to be aimed for are: the Christian development of the new congregation, its strengthening through the effort of winning its relatives, and its enlargement by a series of other group conversions from amongst its own people. A group conversion church properly cared for multiplies within its own people. This is the New Testament type of church growth, for at least a dozen years after it started.

What are the elements of good spiritual nurture of beginning people movements? These have been spoken of again and again throughout the book. Here we shall summarize some of the more important.

Training in worship: The rich meaningful worship of the Christian Church is the birthright of every Christian group. Daily worship of God is invaluable in the achievement of Christian consciousness. For village churches in Mid-India worship should be such that illiterates readily understand and regularly participate in it. This means worship in which memorized materials—prayers, statements of faith, commands, pledges, and confessions—will be used again and again in a simple and generally accepted liturgy. We are not speaking of the worship at the mission station church, where much leadership is available and worshippers are able to read Bible and hymn book. Rich worship in the central station does the illiterate villager no good and is no substitute for meaningful worship among the people movement congregations. The new Christian groups are where the battle will be won or lost. They should be trained till their worship is regular, inspiring, well attended and participated in by all.

Daily worship involves a church building. At the very beginning this may be simply a sacred spot under a tree, fenced to keep out cattle, goats and pigs; or it may be a village home. Soon it should become a chapel built by the people, probably in the style of a village house, understood to be theirs, used daily and honoured as the place of worship. Missions frequently aid in building such chapels, though if the congregation can erect their chapel they by all means should do so.

Honorary local leaders: Amongst the first duties of those to whom God has committed the spiritual care of a beginning people movement is that of discovering, training, and keeping at work its honorary leaders. In addition to brief annual periods of training, responsibility for conducting evening worship, preparing enquirers, and attending monthly leaders meetings, should be laid on them. People learn by doing. The missionary cannot hope personally to teach 5000 Christians; but he can teach the leaders of twice that number.

A paid pastorate. The best of the people being saved should be trained both as catechists and as ministers. Within a few years after the first groups have been baptized, catechists out of the people movement should be at work. Ordained ministers of the people itself should be available within a few years more. To be avoided are training centers, rural or urban, which make their graduate, unwilling to go back amongst their own people, to live in humble village fashion, marry girls of their own clans and in short to identify themselves with their own people.

We have been impressed with the primary importance of training leaders from among the people being discipled. Only these know their congregations well enough to shepherd them. Only these, as a rule, feel thoroughly at home with them. The son of an urban central station church has a very great adjustment to make out in some distant village. He is a foreigner to them, even if he is Indian to the core. He may have to be used in the very beginning, but he should be superseded by "leaders out of the movement" as soon as these can be trained.

Planned giving to the Church: Pickett's studies revealed that an average of two rupees per annum per family in 1930 was a reasonable objective in most rural churches. The habit of such giving will not establish itself. It must be taught as God's provision for His Church. As rapidly as possible catechists and pastors who are dependent on the gifts of the Christians should be appointed to the congregations. Often they will have to earn a part of their living as farmers or teachers, or in some other manner. Sometimes in small new groups, especially when in a beginning movement all the persuasion of the older congregations is needed to induce a group to try the Christian way, it will be necessary for the mission to subsidize the village pastor. But this should be recognized by congregations, pastors, church, and mission as a temporary expedient.

Christian truth: Much Christian truth will be learned through daily worship, which provides a regular means of teaching the Bible to the adults. It is the adults who must be taught. At no place does the central station tradition mislead more effectively than in its assumption that the

chief task is teaching children. In people movement churches, teaching children who then go back to a community
of untaught and unchanged adults is largely a waste
of effort. The unconscious life of the adult group is a very
effective school in any village. Where this adult life is at
variance with the conscious program of the mission school,
the latter always suffers and too often is largely neutralized.
Christian truth should be taught to both adults and children in worship, special instruction, institutes and by other
means.

Christian customs: Christian burial, marriage, festivals, symbols, pictures, greetings, postures in worship,
attitudes toward the castes, treatment of women and children—in regard to all these Christian customs need to be
established. Here again wise leadership will avoid forcing
central station customs onto people movement Christians.
Indigenous customs are often quite good. Minor changes in
a few cases may be needed to bring them into harmony
with world-wide Christian sentiment. Central station
Christians could not usually be induced to depart from
the Europeanized customs which they learned from the missionaries as the community was slowly built up but there
is no reason for the new congregations to be tied up to such
foreign customs.

Christian witness: This is one of the most important
functions of the new young people movement churches.
To provide opportunity for them to witness to their faith
is essential. Converts are showered with words of contempt,
blame, and hate. "You have ruined yourselves." "You
have betrayed us." "You have sent seven generations of
ancestors to hell." "You have made a second father."
These are among the milder common abuses which the new

convert must hear. "What did you get out of it" is certain to be said to him. It is assumed in most places in Mid-India that only one in desperate circumstances would betray the faith and become a Christian. Even those who approve of the course taken, express their approval in damning terms "Everyone has to look after his stomach, of course. You did the best you could in hard circumstances" was said to a recent convert in our hearing. All this provides a marvellous opportunity for witness— for the instructed convert. For the poor fellow who has to meet it without preparation, it can be a deadening experience. Then too, after the first weeks or months of reaction are over, the group of converts is constantly faced with caste fellows who are intensely interested in the fact that "our folk have become Christian." They may hate it. They may like it. But they will not be indifferent to it. Few central station Christians have the opportunity for potent witness that is the privilege of the average people movement Christian. No where will deepening and purifying Christian experience yield richer results. For all these reasons the new convert should be taught to bear his witness clear and unwavering in the midst of the kind of comment which his own villagers are likely to make. Teaching new Christians the faith and leading them to witness in terminology which will meet the thought life of their peers is an essential element in early spiritual nurture.

Thus group conversions may be expected to multiply the churches. It was out of living groups and Christian nurture similar to that herein depicted that the great Churches of India have arisen. In "Church Growth and Group Conversion" we have tried to deal with the relationship of people movements to the Central Station Tradition. We have seen central station churches and missions: (a) with no group ingathering whatever, (b) with well handled possibilities of group ingathering, (c) with mis-handled possibilities of group conversions, (d) with people movements well under way and then arrested, and (e) with people movement Churches growing from strength to strength. In this last chapter we have considered how the Church grows when it grows greatly, how such growth starts in fresh fields and in those where the central station pattern has been stamped in, and finally how new young people movements may best be shepherded.

Readers will by the years be divided into two parts— those who give intellectual assent to the argument and then continue to practice elements of the Central Station Tradition; and those who spare no pains to learn the people movement pattern, teach it to others and prayerfully work that "churches which can grow" may come into being. To these latter readers, this book is dedicated with confidence that all labour to win the peoples of this earth to Christ is in line with the will of God and that the day of people movements to Christian faith is just beginning,— from all castes, and tribes and kindreds and peoples.